Under a Dark Eye

Sicilian Campa[ign?]
August 5, 19[4?]

Dear Glad,

Are you ready to chalk up
completion of another one? I am, ju[st]
about.

Three more days will mark [my]
9th month over seas. It does seem a[s]
though we have been away from the [states?]
for a long long time. Although t[he]
time over here fairly flies, if you [know]
what I mean. Without papers or [radio?]
we seldom if ever know what day [of]
the week it is. Often times, upon [?]
inquiring for the date, we are surpr[ised]
to find that a week has slipped by, [a]
month almost spent, or a season [?]
This is primarily due to the fact, tha[t we]
seldom stay at any one place very lo[ng]
and there has been a constant change [of]
scenery, with new adventures and
[s]peculations, in the offing. One m[ight]
say that we have earned the tit[le]

Under a Dark Eye *A Family Story*

Sharon Dunn

Letter from Sicily, first page, August 5, 1943

Texas Tech University Press

This book is typeset in Centaur. The paper used in this book meets the minimum requirements of ANSI/NISO Z39.48-1992 (R1997). ♾

Cover photograph provided by the author

Library of Congress Cataloging-in-Publication Data
Names: Dunn, Sharon, 1946- author.
Title: Under a dark eye : a family story / Sharon Dunn.
Description: Lubbock, Texas : Texas Tech University Press, 2017. | Includes
   bibliographical references and index.
Identifiers: LCCN 2016048477 (print) | LCCN 2016050728 (ebook) | ISBN
   9780896729858 (hardcover : alkaline paper) | ISBN 9780896729865 (paperback
   : alkaline paper) | ISBN 9780896729872 (ebook)
Subjects: LCSH: Dunn, Sharon, 1946---Family. | Dunn, Sharon, 1946——Childhood
   and youth. | Dunn, Gilbert, 1910-1972. | Ward-Dunn, Gladys, 1907-1980. |
   Adult children of dysfunctional families—United States—Biography. |
   Parents—New Hampshire—Concord—Biography. | Abusive men—New
   Hampshire—Concord—Biography. | Women psychiatrists—New
   Hampshire—Concord—Biography. | Married people—New
   Hampshire—Concord—Biography. | New Hampshire State Hospital—Biography.
Classification: LCC CT275.D882265 A3 2017 (print) | LCC CT275.D882265 (ebook)
   | DDC 974.2/72—dc23
LC record available at https://lccn.loc.gov/2016048477

17 18 19 20 21 22 23 24 25 / 9 8 7 6 5 4 3 2 1

Texas Tech University Press
Box 41037 | Lubbock, Texas 79409-1037 USA
800.832.4042 | ttup@ttu.edu | www.ttupress.org

From *Refugees in the Garden*, Rose Press, 2009: "The Pyramids," "Mail Order," "Refugees in the Garden," "Family Business," "Working Mother," "Mother's Tongue," "The Kitchen Table Tells Its Tale," "Last Months"

From *My Brother and I*, Finishing Line Press, 2012: "Spring Rain," "Anna Lived with Us," "His Work," "Daddy's Girl," "25 South Main Street"

for
Michael Dunn
Aaron Clayton-Dunn
Mary Carmen Ward Earle

My deep appreciation to Jacqueline Kolosov for her mentorship and to Zane Kotker and Martha Collins for their abiding support. Thank you to dear family and friends for reading and for conversations. And thanks to Naomi Czekaj-Robbins of the Wellfleet Public Library for help with research. Finally, with more gratitude than I can ever express to John J. Clayton for his encouragement.

It would appear, he often used to say to himself, that children never ask themselves any questions. Many years afterwards, we attempt to solve puzzles that were not mysteries at the time and we try to decipher half-obliterated letters from a language that is too old and whose alphabet we don't even know.

—**Patrick Modiano,** *So You Don't Get Lost in the Neighborhood*

The past beats inside me like a second heart.

—**John Banville,** *The Sea*

The search after meaning is especially insidious because it always succeeds.

—**Donald Spence,** *Narrative Truth and Historical Truth*

Contents

Prologue

I began this book wanting to find an answer to a single question: what made my father into the complex, unempathetic man I knew? He cast a deep shadow on my and my brother's childhoods and on into our adulthood. As I went through Gilbert Dunn's life, reconstructing it through his photographs and writing, my own research, and my memories and those of others, I arrived at a much larger, and illuminating, view of the forces that played on his life and shaped his mind.

Along the way, though, I realized that I needed to see the ways my psychiatrist mother figured in the story. How did she come to marry this man? Why did she stay in her marriage? Did she truly understand the effect of her husband on their children? So, after finishing up my father's life, I plunged into researching Gladys Ward's. Thus, the two sections of this book.

It takes a Philadelphia law
where our stands these days
ire du cœur. I have I be
against the postal authoriti
piring to contribute to the
ffections of a global battle
believe that's what I am. If
tainly "out of bounds." I
you ain't" is not a foolish
what I'm waiting to

In my last letter I
a little of China. What
have seen — but which is to-da
per. From the air the co
the most beautiful spectacle
seen. The entire landscap
sweeping graceful curves o
igated vegetation. Rice pl
is water laden beds appear

The Search for My Father

Part One

Letter from China, page two, August 15, 1944

I: The Search

Years ago, summertime, I was house-sitting in Peterborough, New Hampshire, for a writer and her husband who had taken their young daughters to Spain for a month. I welcomed the family home in late evening and stayed one last night. It was early, I was sipping coffee at the breakfast table, and the father and one of the two girls, she was about twelve, were talking in low tones at the kitchen sink. A window backlit them. They talked about ten minutes. He listened to her closely; she was upset. Bending over, he answered her and he listened more. She cried; he said a few more words. Finally this father put an arm around his daughter, one hand behind her head, fingers woven through her dark hair, pressing her to his chest.

I was thirty years old, and I did not know firsthand that such a relationship could exist between father and child. My heart clenched in longing. Soon the rest of the family made their entrances, ready for orange juice, toast, good-byes. In a daze I loaded the car and headed out.

My father had died six years earlier. A tyrant at home, he seemed all-powerful because the lens of childhood magnifies. I never had a real conversation with him—and I was an adult when he died. I hated him for how he unceasingly disparaged my younger brother and disdained our mother all my childhood. And I loved him—for his handsome face, his trim neatness in chinos and plaid shirts, for how good I felt when he approved of me—for my top grades, my subdued presence, and my continual efforts to please him. Though I majored in English literature in college and landed my first job with a New York trade book publisher—on the way to my dream of being a book editor—I ended up working over thirty-five years with my brother in the business our father started in 1952 and ran alone until lung cancer overtook him in 1971. During his life it was a one-man business that never made money; Mike and I grew it a hundredfold, built it into a stable local employer, profitable, with national sales and a national reputation. We credited our father as the founder of this success—this father who never had business success, and who had certainly never been a success as a father.

My father, as I knew him in the last third of his sixty-two years, had no friends. We lived on the grounds of the New Hampshire State Hospital in Concord, in a brick duplex provided as part of my mother's compensation as clinical director, the psychiatrist in charge of outpatient clinics for the entire state. Most of the other husbands and fathers living in staff housing were psychiatrists, often with intellectual interests beyond their profession. In the immediate post–World War II years, the NHSH recruited many physicians who were refugees from war-ravaged Europe—from Lithuania, Latvia, Estonia, Yugoslavia, Hungary, Ukraine—most fleeing the iron fist of the Soviet Union, many having suffered displacement or worse at the hands of the Nazis. These doctors were multilingual, and they enjoyed ballet and opera in Boston with their families. My father had nothing in common with any of the physicians who were my mother's colleagues.

Gilbert Dunn did not graduate from high school, was not a reader. How different it would have been for him socially if he were, say, a lawyer with a practice in downtown Concord, or an engineer, or an architect, or a teacher. He would have had a profession. Instead, his status was more or less the same as a housewife—and this was the late 1940s, the early 1950s, when it was men who *worked*, defined themselves by their work.

Our father spent those first four years in New Hampshire at home, in a basement workshop, trying to invent a product. He finally came upon an idea with promise—a bird-feeding station that offered seed and water and clipped to a wooden windowsill for close-up viewing of backyard birds. In 1952 he rented space seven miles away in a village called Penacook, where he worked alone, making his wooden bird feeders in his own small assembly line. He placed small advertisements in newspapers and magazines and began shipping orders. At least now he could say that he ran his own business. But he knew that his one-man enterprise was struggling, that his wife's salary financed it. Gil Dunn belonged to no clubs, no church. He fished alone. He went to work every morning, he came home every evening to read the newspaper, drink a highball, eat dinner, watch TV, and go to bed.

Is it surprising our father ruled the household? His installation came about partly because for so long he was the parent at home while our mother worked. In the early years my mother, I am sure, thought this man needed a place where he was "somebody." However, he took over permanently, in ways large and small, so that the household pivoted around him and we obeyed his rules. We ate only what he liked: never cheese, no nuts in any foods. Though we never had bread and butter at dinner, he insisted the table be set with bread and butter plates and butter knives. All the state hospital buildings were steam-heated from a central plant, and heat was provided at no charge, yet he ordered us to turn off the bedroom radiator at night. Mike and I woke up on winter mornings to ice inside our windows and scrambled in the freezing cold to dress. Did this contribute to our many colds and earaches in grade school? Perhaps. Or was the constant cigarette haze from two chain-smokers the cause? And, of course, our father was our disciplinarian.

Spring Rain

We are bad children,
bad, bad children
sent to our room
again and again
up the stairs
down the short hall,
door shut,
into silence.

Today the rain calls to us
through our window,
sprinkling in
on arms, faces
through the screen
where tiny squares
bead with water.
We run our nails down
to draw water pictures,

rivers of rain.
Our tongues taste, rain
splatters on our cheeks,
we daub it, flick it,
it smells so fresh
on that breeze.

"Close that window."
He stands there,
hands open:
a chocolate in each.
Water pools on the sill.
Obediently we lower
the wet window,
watch his hands close,
door shut,
into silence.

What it was like in our house: Our mother was at work all day, getting home sometime between 5:15 and 6:00. Our father drove home from "the shop" around 5:30 and parked his car in the garage out back. He climbed the back steps and entered the kitchen with his briefcase. He made highballs for the two of them, and often drank another jigger of whiskey before closing the cabinet door. In the living room he read the *Concord Monitor*, and Mother worked on the day's crossword. Soon our housekeeper Anna peered around the corner, wiping her damp hands on her apron: "Na, dinner is ready."

Mike and I came downstairs to the dining room: damask tablecloth and napkins; sterling silver flatware; abundant food in serving dishes clustered near our father's place. I sat opposite my brother and saw his face; behind him was a large mirror in which I saw my face. Every evening our father found something wrong with Mike, who was four, five, seven, or ten or thirteen . . . At six he squirmed trying to cut his meat, and our father stared: "When are you going to learn to use a knife?" Mike's back was touching the chair back. "Chair backs are not made for leaning on," our father said. "Sit up straight." Why wasn't his napkin in his lap? Was this behavior deliberate? "Are you mocking me?" Now Mike sat too close to the table. He didn't move the chair back gently, the legs caught on the carpet. He was gulping his food. The topics of criticism evolved as we grew older. Mike's grades, C's and D's. His hair too long, his shirt not tucked in. Every night, relentless, year after year. I tried to start conversations about Daddy's work at the shop or what happened at school, I asked him to pass the salt, but nothing truly distracted him. Mike's spoon clattered against a dish and chastisement began. A few times, I remember, Mother left the room crying, napkin crumpled on her seat, and then we were left alone with our father, which felt very lonely. Over the years the room was papered in yellow roses, then in pale blue diamonds, finally painted white. Sometimes I thought we would be in this room forever. The dinner table was the central dramatic setting of our lives: my father, driven by a dark power, focused on the minutiae of my brother's every move and word.

After those tense and bitter dinners, our father watched television in the living room, seated on the couch next to an end table with an ashtray overflowing. Strangely, Mike and I could then be in the room with him without strife. *The Huntley-Brinkley Report, Bonanza, Maverick, Gunsmoke,* and *The Jackie Gleason Show*—they soothed him. Mother sat in her upholstered chair, also smoking, reading a detective novel or lacquering her long nails. It was as if TV were a cool oasis, shimmering, our respite from the dry storm inside him that seeped out and abraded us invisibly day by day.

My father went off to work, including most Saturdays, and made contact with a few vendors on the telephone, or spoke with folks who stopped by the small storefront to buy birdseed or other items that were also sold in the mail-order catalog he eventually created. He worked alone except for seasonal shippers he hired in the late fall. Summers were slow, and often he knocked off in the afternoon to go fishing on the Merrimack River. We knew this because he would come home with perch, mackerel, or fat river bass for Anna to descale, then cook for dinner. There was an emptiness about his fatherhood, a gray emotional frost that settled in our house. His only heat was his anger: he could not offer another warmth—of arms, of a loving eye, of real knowing.

In contrast, Mother's world out of the house was peopled with scores of patients and their families, nurses, other doctors, and social workers. Beside her living room chair there was often a foot-high stack of patient files for her to review. She handed over her paycheck to her husband, and most of it he invested in the fledgling manufacturing and mail-order business. A few evenings each week she walked across the street after dinner to the Thayer Building to her office to treat private patients. She kept the private therapy fees to buy clothes for herself and for Mike and me.

When my brother Mike was seven years old, our mother transcribed several of his dreams. After she died I came across them jotted in pencil in a notebook among her things. This dream was dated November 1954. I can hear my little brother's voice.

> One day there was this little flower planted in the desert. It didn't have any water so it almost died. But the little flower had legs so it walked and walked and walked. Then it met a tree. The tree didn't have any water. So the little flower said to the big tree, "Won't you come with me? Maybe we can find some water. Then maybe we can live instead of die." The tree, as you probably know, has legs too. And so they walked and walked and walked. On and on they went until they saw a pump near a little log house. They started the pump but no water was in it. It was all dried up. So they walked until they came to a wooden house with a pump near it. They tried that pump but they couldn't get a drop of water. So on they went and they came to a brick house. People were living there but they were cruel and didn't give the flower or the tree any water. Then they walked and walked and walked until they came to a little town. It was haunted and there was a big well in the middle of the haunted town. There was lots and lots of water in it. They drank to their hearts' content.

The haunted town is like the dream world itself, where the two living "beings" search together to find a well—with *wished-for* water—that is, sustenance and love . . . where they can drink their fill. Mike's dream is my evidence that he felt, as I always have, that we were bonded in our childhood's journey. That bond has been one of the very strongest in my life.

Our mother had also kept Mike's pencil-on-paper portraits of our father and himself, drawn around the same time. Mike's portrait of our father shows a large downturned mouth, two scowl lines across the forehead, pinpoint-pupil round eyes surrounded by wire glasses, a hand holding a report card with U's (for Unsatisfactory—our grade school only had S and U), on his sweater an *H* and on his hat (with feather) another *H*. I suspect that the *H*

My brother's portrait of our father and his self-portrait, with our mother's pen notations "DADDY" (left) and "Mike Himself."

stands for *Hate.* I am sure that my brother felt that my father hated him.

The more I look at my brother's drawing of himself, the more I see stoicism in the flat lines of his mouth. Drawing mouth, eyes, and low brows, Mike pressed the pencil down hard and dark on the paper; his forehead lines are like his father's; and, as for the spattering of freckles, which blond Mike had like pale stars, those on the right in the drawing look like tears falling in a straight line.

What did my mother, a psychiatrist, make of these products of her young son's mind? Could she not see how her husband was damaging Mike? If she did fully realize the meaning of dream and drawings, did she ultimately judge that it was better to have Gil in the family than to be a single professional woman trying to raise two children? Did she believe it was better for us to have a father, even this father, than no father? My mind has run in circles. I know how little my father contributed to family life. He did as little as possible with us children before we were five, and less after that; he used our home like a hotel; and as man and wife our parents had no intimate life, I believe, and very little companionable time. Was it that my mother could not face the opprobrium of divorce in the 1950s? Had she determined that without our family, without her support, Gil would have a failed life—no business, no work, only his unhappy failed self—and she could not bear to have responsibility for that outcome?

It was only when I myself was older than my father when he died, when I had retired after more than thirty years from the business my father started and ran for twenty years by himself, that I could face the question of why my father was the irritable, critical, unhappy, and negative man I knew. Was working all those years and growing my father's business my unconscious way of being close to him, even in death—when he could not be close to me in life, never listened to me, or dried my tears, or held me to his chest with his large, freckled hands? And is my writing this a similar attempt at closeness? Perhaps.

But this is crucial: By the time I retired I had accomplished two unspoken missions. First, the success of the business redeemed our failed father, in my eyes, and, second, my brother was safe, ensconced in a work environment where he was thriving and appreciated. Now I had the emotional energy, the drive, to investigate and reconstruct the life of this complex, difficult man of whom I knew so very little and who had had such an impact on my entire life. His genealogy, the times and events he lived through, his sorrows, his interests, even passions—these would shape a story, a fuller story of the life of Gilbert Dunn. I hoped finally to know my father.

And I hoped that when I had unearthed my father's past and imagined his emotional landscape, that my anger against him could dissipate, and that my childhood, its central mystery in the light, would cease to haunt me, could loosen its grip and let me go.

2: Gil's Youth

I set myself on a journey to reconstruct my father's life, learn about and imagine the years when I did not know him. I wanted to understand how he came to be the father I knew, the man I feared and somehow still loved. What transformed this smiling boy in knickers into the brittle unhappy man that I experienced as a daughter?

Gil, age nine.

Many years ago I found a small yellowed photograph of my father as a boy. I fell in love with it because its spirit surprised me so. I had a negative made from the print and framed an enlargement of the image, as a talisman. Looking at it I could conjure an earlier version of this soul, as yet uncorrupted. The happiness on this boy's face, my father's face, was priceless to me. He was out of doors, filled with pride, perhaps even joy. Now I would summon all my research skills to track him through the years, to dig into his experiences and extract their emotional import and effect on his spirit.

How would I learn about the early years of my father's life, when I did not know him, and when so few stories of the past were shared? I had only these bare facts: Gil Dunn grew up in New York City, worked on Wall Street, sold Hoover vacuum cleaners, and served in World War II. But the flesh of his experience, the real story? What shed the most light on his youth and early adulthood ended up in my hands after my parents' deaths—two albums and a small suitcase. I had looked through them briefly years ago, but now I pondered them obsessively, sometimes with a magnifying glass in hand.

The first album was Gil's, started when he was sixteen in 1926. It is half-filled with over a hundred black-and-white photos mounted on black pages, many with his handwritten captions. The album stops when he was twenty-eight. So, these photographs gave me entry into twelve years.

The other album was my mother's, where she collected colorful postcards Gil sent her during his service overseas in World War II. He often wrote a letter on a series of ten or more postcards of, say, beautiful Italian peasant women or of wildflowers.

During the war Gil carried a small suitcase from country to country. On its light tan leather top surface, he inked, in artful lettering, over a hundred names of islands, battles, cities, towns, rivers, seas, oceans, and sights he had seen. The suitcase, when I took possession of it, bulged with handwritten letters, pages of a journal, and an application for commission as an officer—with the only detailed record I have of his employment history. Little notebooks listed military postings and work assignments; small wallets held photos, newspaper classifieds, train ticket stubs, travel orders back to the States, meal tickets for a hospital in Kentucky, and a copy of his honorable discharge. Gil's letters, over thirty of them, and scores of his postcards, were those he wrote my mother; so either he or she stored them there. Unfortunately, only three of her wartime letters to him are included, and I will never know if that is because he did not keep her letters, or because he or she tossed them out later.

Over the years I came across paperwork I felt I should not discard, and it turned out these added to the story. I salvaged tax returns from the late 1940s and 1950s, drawings of inventions my father tried to patent, and a mostly empty notebook in which my mother had made cryptic jottings, such as codes for hospital emergencies—where she had written down Mike's dreams and slipped in those drawings. In a shoebox I had squirreled away letters from my college years. Another shoebox held hundreds of miscellaneous family photos and a mystery packet of negatives.

The range and detail of information I found online amazed me. US Census data revealed my grandfather Martin Dunn's ethnicity, which he had refused to tell me—100 percent Irish. Knowing that, I could access Irish Roman Catholic parish records to try to locate our Dunn ancestors. Which county in Ireland? Trial and error, days spent, but I finally ended up in the on-line parish records of Monasterevin, County Kildare, where names and birth years matched those in the 1870 US Census. Yes, these were the Dunns who immigrated to New York City in the mid-1800s. I was excited to track back to 1820, to my grandfather's grandfather's birth, to discover his name was Martin Dunne and to realize how many generations bore the name Martin, either as a first name or a middle name: my grandfather, my father, my brother, my brother's son, my brother's grandson.

Online I found photos of P-40 planes, the kind my father worked on, ships he boarded, newsreel clips of the victory parade in Tunis he marched in. I tracked down a two-volume memoir-history by a pilot in my father's Army Air Forces fighter group, and a crucial book about AAF convalescent hospitals. All these materials and sources, along with conversations with my brother and my aunt, and my own memories, came together for me to construct Gil Dunn's story.

My quest for information about my family started early. The summer I turned fifteen I interviewed my father's parents about their families of origin. My grandmother Rose Dunn told me that she was the daughter of Scandinavian immigrants—father Danish, mother Swedish. They settled in the Bronx, and at sixteen Rose Ehlers had worked as a milliner. She described her father as a slacker, who hid under the bedcovers when social services knocked on the door. I never asked how she met Martin Dunn, whom she married at eighteen in 1909. When I turned and asked my grandfather about his family, he said, "What do you want to know that for?"

Discovering that my grandfather Martin was 100 percent Irish was my

1913: Rose, twenty-two, and son Gilbert, three.

first research victory and showed me that my tenacity could pay off with a new fact. His mother was born of Irish immigrants, and his father Maurice (pronounced "Morris") Dunn was born in Ireland—this information was right there in the 1900 US Census. The Irish were discriminated against in the mid-to-late 1800s, and this could be the reason for my grandfather's obdurate silence. Martin had eight siblings; he was the second son and the first to leave the tenement on West 123rd St. in Manhattan to set off on his own.

In 1910 at age nineteen, Rose gave birth to Gilbert Martin Dunn, my father, the first of her two children. That year Gilbert's father, Martin, twenty-five, was working as a bookkeeper for the New York Telephone Company, the first of many positions he held in his long career there. An early photo of Gil shows a smiling child.

First Rose and Martin Dunn lived in the Bronx, at two addresses; then they moved to Manhattan, where I tracked four more addresses over twenty years, each more northerly.

By 1918 when Gil was eight, the family lived on West 147th Street in Harlem, at that time predominantly populated by Italian and other European immigrants, including a large proportion of Jews. As Harlem filled with poorer immigrants and African Americans, the Dunns next moved to an area now called Inwood in northernmost Manhattan, first on Vermilyea Avenue, then Sherman Avenue. As the 1930s rolled on, Inwood itself became a magnet for German Jews. Gil had many lifelong ethnic prejudices against Italians, blacks, and Jews, prejudices perhaps fueled by resentment of his family's many moves. Gil lived there at the top of Manhattan from age fourteen until he was in his midtwenties.

Can I imagine his life in those years?

As I opened Gil's photograph album this time, I was looking for the story the photos would tell me. In his late teens and early twenties I saw him surrounded by so many buddies. They lie on pebbly river beaches, hang out on docks, pose with canoe paddles on the shore. I see that as a young man Gil was no loner. The Island Canoe Club of City Island in the Bronx was the center of his social life. In all kinds of weather he and his friends paddled for pleasure and also in races organized by clubs, the American Canoe Association, and by the city of New York.

Gil's friend and fellow Island Canoe Club member Charles Fay twice won the Around Manhattan canoe marathon, in 1930 and 1934—it takes about

Winter 1929: Ed, Gil, Jack, Sandy.

*1930: Gil, top, second from left,
hands on Edna's shoulders.*

five and a half hours to paddle all the rivers and channels. Gil was there at
the finish in 1930, cheering. He himself was on the winning team for the
four-man single paddle in the 1931 Long Island Canoe Championship, in the
junior division. Canoeing was Gil's year-round passion. Not far behind were
swimming (a sport he also raced in) and camping.

Gil put into his album photos of young men and women in bathing suits,
arms around each other. Individual portraits of many young women fill the
early pages—Blanche, Lil, May, Mickey, Frenchie, Ruth. Who is the Gil Dunn
I see here? An athletic vigorous young man who has an array of friends—
Don, Ray, Bughouse, Jack, Sandy, Ed, Larry, and at least two girlfriends—
Edna and later Kay.

I pieced together the few hard specifics of Gil's education and his early
work history from two sets of forms he filled out years later for the Army,
stored in his small suitcase. He had left George Washington High School in
Washington Heights after only one year. Gil had been headed toward a career
in commercial art—he excelled at drafting (the only subject he liked) and had
an extraordinarily beautiful freehand script. The following is a rare story he

told us himself and for that reason I think it very significant. One day in class he illustrated a dog's reddish brown spots—in green ink. Not only was he was shamed by the hilarity of his classmates, he was disheartened. His profound color blindness precluded success, he was told, in the only area he had interest in. This was a major disappointment—and he turned his back on school. In that era, in his social environment, leaving before graduating was not un- common, nor looked down upon. Neither of his parents were educated—for instance, his father started work when he was nine—so Gil's departure from school was acceptable. Still, I pause at this early disappointment: Gil's hope foiled through no fault of his own, but by a gene inherited from his mother.

To Wall Street at Sixteen

In 1926 Gil began working as a messenger at the stock brokerage firm Dyer, Hudson & Co. at 36 Wall Street, and it is no coincidence that this is the year he started his photograph album. How many sixteen-year-olds back then "documented" their lives? Does the fact that Gil took and kept photos mean that he felt his life was worth documenting, a life to be proud of in recollec- tion?

But how did Gil land this "plum" job as a runner on Wall Street? I em- barked on the trail to answer that question when I became curious about a photo from the shoebox stuffed with miscellaneous old family photos. Inside a tent a soldier sat on a bench reading. Who was this? With my magnifying glass I deciphered a small sign posted in the ground outside: *Capt. Dunn.* I had vaguely known my grandfather Martin was at one point "Captain Dunn," but I knew nothing about his service, not even which branch of the military.

Online I was able to find out that Martin Dunn joined the New York National Guard as a private in 1906, the year it was established. He served forty-three years, participating in all weekend and weeklong summer trainings until mandatory retirement. His Guard duty was obviously a serious avocation that Martin managed along with a dedicated career and family life. By the time Gil was in high school, his father Martin had risen to lieutenant on staff in the inner circle of General George R. Dyer of the 87th Brigade. In 1925 the *New York Times* reported that Dyer had become the head of a Wall Street brokerage firm. Aha! The Dyer, Hudson firm hires young Gil Dunn, son of General Dyer's trusted staffer—and that was how a boy from the top of Manhattan landed a job on Wall Street thirteen miles south from home.

What a time for a young man to be working on Wall Street! The New York Stock Exchange was booming, fortunes were being made. Messengers like Gil effected the trades, running from brokerage houses to the exchanges. In the heated market there was so much business that employers demanded the boys work long hours, and sometimes they had to stay overnight on cots in the office. (Gil's commute from the Dyckman Street station to Wall Street took about forty minutes each way.) Young Gil Dunn was in the thick of this remarkable activity and could not help but be optimistic about the future. Oddly, my father recounted only two details, in a rather minor key, of his Wall Street years. The first was, how in order to eat at lunch counters, he had to hold his arms in tight to his body in the crush of diners. And he started smoking then at sixteen, a habit he never broke.

On a spring weekend in 1929, in his third year working on Wall Street, Gil suffered an accident that would have lifelong effects. He overturned his racing canoe in the polluted waters of the Hudson River and contracted spinal meningitis, an acute inflammation of the protective membranes of the brain and spinal cord. The survival rate from this disease was 50 percent. In this era prior to the advent of sulfa drugs and antibiotics, the only treatment for spinal meningitis was serotherapy: puncturing the lumbar spine, extracting spinal fluid, and replacing it with a serum formulated from horses who had had meningitis. The treatment was administered at twelve-hour intervals, for a total of approximately eighteen punctures. Constant nursing was required, first in hospital, later at home. Just that winter Gil's two younger cousins—the sons of his mother's only brother—had drowned after falling through the ice while skating. I can imagine Rose's fears for her son. But after enduring a debilitating illness, and its painful treatment, nineteen-year-old Gil was perched, smiling, on a bicycle at a cabin on Lake Cossayuna upstate. He recuperated with his family during their annual freshwater summer holiday

However, the bout with spinal meningitis marked Gil for life. Not only did he lose a season of competitive canoeing, but the life-threatening illness took the edge off his robust physicality in the short term. It was his friend Charlie Fay who was able to race his canoe around Manhattan in 1930, not Gil. And a longer-term effect was likely to have been permanent damage to his nervous system: some survivors of spinal meningitis were known to experience lowered libido and sexual dysfunction.

Convalescing at Lake Cossayuna, 1929.

Gil and his mother Rose, 1930.

Margin clerk on Wall Street, 1930.

A photo from the following summer shows Gil and his mother Rose sitting together on a rock near water. He is twenty, she is thirty-eight. She is touching his hand in the most loving way, and you can sense their closeness. Nursing him through his grave illness brought them closer than ever, and I imagine she was proud of him, this son who was working downtown, making a career for himself, and visiting his vacationing family on rocky Esopus Island in the Hudson on the weekend.

Crash and Decline of the Stock Market

Although Gil Dunn's illness and convalescence took him away from Dyer, Hudson for several months in the spring and summer of 1929, this absence did not affect his employment. However, a shock was on its way for Gil and the rest of the country. In late October 1929 the hyperventilated stock market crashed. Dyer, Hudson, like most brokerage houses, I was surprised to find

Gil sailing toward Edna, 1930.

out, was *not* put out of business, and Gil remained employed. The market actually recovered shakily over the next year. By 1930 Gil had been promoted to margin clerk—he kept track of over two thousand accounts where stocks were bought with borrowed funds, bought with the confidence that stock prices would always rise higher.

Stocks might fall, investors reasoned, but they always regained and went higher, didn't they? Gil's portrait from 1930 shows a well-dressed young man—in three-piece suit, silk tie. At twenty, he already had thinning hair.

And Gil had a girlfriend, Edna Mallon, who was in an earlier group photo. In one photograph a smiling Edna posed in a bathing suit. Gil mounted that photo on a cardboard holder, inked the surround, and lettered her name and the year, 1930. He glued a smaller photo of himself sailing toward her. I would say he was in love with her.

Another photograph held special significance for my father. Enlarged and hand-colored, this 1931 portrait was framed and hung in a passageway in our house when I was growing up. Looking much older than his twenty-one years,

January 1931, near Wall Street. Gil will turn twenty-one in February.

Gil is elegantly dressed in topcoat with a velvet collar, derby hat, white scarf, and leather gloves. He holds a camera, a symbol of affluence at that time. He and a friend took photos of each other, and I expect right then on that January day in 1931 they were still bullish about their future. After all that had happened on Wall Street, they still had their jobs. This was perhaps the high point of his life: he had a good job, he had a love.

I noticed how well Gil dressed. When I knew him decades later he still had a large collection of colorful geometric silk ties, purchased in his Wall Street days. This young man was making money. Did he invest his savings? His employer General Dyer was quoted in a bulletin from Barron's Boston News Bureau: "Anyone who buys our highest-class rails and industrials, including the steels, coppers and utilities, and holds them, will make a great deal of money." Investing must have seemed a sure thing.

But another, much longer, steady slide of the stock market began, from April 1931 until July 8, 1932, when the market closed at the lowest level of the twentieth century. It was in 1932, the year the Dow lost 90 percent of its value, that Gil Dunn lost his position at Dyer, Hudson.

Gil experienced a profound and painful change in worldview. Life as he knew it would never be the same. The foundation he thought he was building in those six years at Dyer, Hudson had crumbled. For the rest of his days he never paid any attention to the stock market; you would have never known that he had been immersed in Wall Street. If Gil had invested his own savings in the market as General Dyer recommended, his financial loss would have made this time even more painful.

The Depression Digs In

Gil would be out of work almost three years, until sometime in 1935. I am sure he looked for work and couldn't find it. What effect did unemployment have on his romantic life? Did Edna decide the out-of-work Gil was not for her, did she find a man who still had a job in this difficult time? Or did something else go wrong between them? There were no more photos of Edna in Gil's album.

Starting in 1932 there were changes in the album: no longer captions or dates on any photo, no more individual portraits of young women. However, one photo chronicles a festive occasion amid the Depression. December 1933 marked the end of Prohibition. In an apartment Gil and friends gathered

Gil in December 1933, celebrating the end of Prohibition. He is in the middle, teacup in hand.

around card tables, drank out of teacups, and gripped unlabeled bottles. I recognize two old canoeing pals, Don and Bob, but none of the young women. Gil's auburn hair is now so thin you can see through it to the bald pate he would soon have; he's only twenty-three.

Slipped into Gil's album are yellowed newspaper clippings from the mid-1930s about canoe races—and swim races—where both Gil and his sister, Muriel, were winners. One clipping recorded that Gil Dunn helped organize a regatta, as well as participated in it. So his passion for canoeing, begun in his midteens, was still alive almost ten years later. The effort and pleasure of competition was a productive and healthy outlet. What Gil did with the rest of his time, and especially in winter, I have no way of knowing.

Equally unknowable is Gil's frame of mind in these years, what life inside his family was like. Gil's father, Martin, was not only secure at New York Telephone, where he'd worked since 1906, but had steadily advanced in a career there. New York Telephone was one of the top growth industries of the era. Martin made himself valuable and he was never laid off. Was the long period of Gil's unemployment the beginning of his turning inward? Did he compare himself to his father and come up short? Was Martin Dunn resentful that Gil was not working and that he had to support this able-bodied son?

My belief is that Martin Dunn was hypercritical of his son—and that a stream of scorn has flowed through time from Martin to Gilbert and then to my brother Michael, father to son to son. Perhaps its origin goes back even farther in time. I have one piece of evidence, one piece of evidence alone, of what happened between my grandfather and father. My grandparents were visiting us in New Hampshire, and my grandmother, Rose, witnessed her son Gil bearing down on a young Mike harshly and out of proportion. My mother told me that Rose commented quietly to her: "Just like his father did with him."

This is an occasion when I am leaping, extrapolating on what appears to be slender footing but which I judge as solid. Abusive behavior is a family secret, not a subject a woman and her daughter-in-law sit at the kitchen table and compare notes on. My grandmother and mother went no further than this one communication, neither revealing how much they each had witnessed over the years in their households. "Just like his father did with him." Those seven words are a key to my father's psychology.

I imagine Gil powerless to find work in the worst economic time the country had ever seen. I imagine his mother being loving and supportive, and his father rankling at what he perceived as the coddling of a malingerer. What emotional structures did Gil build to protect himself, to ward off scorn, to get rid of the guilt and shame brewing inside? I cannot know how early in his life his father began giving him a "hard time." If it was early in Gil's life, then the jobless years would have intensified all his self-protective processes.

Finally, in 1935 Gil did land a job with the Hoover Company, which had a growing, aggressive sales organization marketing vacuum cleaners for homes. I've done some supposing: that Martin insisted, "Get a job, any job, or else." Gil at twenty-five was still living with his parents; at the same age Martin Dunn had been out of his parents' home for five years, had settled in at a good job, had married and fathered a child. Gil was not emulating his father's early independence and steps into adult life. Martin knew that and Gil knew that.

When I turn the album's page, there's Gil's business card: he was territory manager, later city sales manager in Yonkers, for the Hoover Company, manufacturers and marketers of vacuum cleaners, a labor-saving household machine that was just beginning to be widely adopted. He photographed one of his sales teams with an award plaque—they had placed second in sales nationally.

Gil, 1937 or so.

Gil managed forty-four salesmen as well as office staff. So, he was promoted, and managing people was one of his skills. He was on the path to success again.

The album's next photos show young people in their late twenties—racing outboard motorboats. We see Gil was still part of a group of friends enjoying the outdoors. He included photos of a stucco house in Mahopac, a half hour north of the city, that his father bought in 1932 and used at first as a weekend getaway while keeping an apartment in Manhattan; the Dunns took up primary residence in Mahopac in the early 1940s. And several photos in summer and winter show Gil with a young woman named Kay.

Among the album's final pictures are those of a roadster. This black shiny vehicle with rumble seat, proud possession of a young man making good money, is parked in the driveway of the Mahopac house. However, in the next images, the roadster is smashed, from a head-on collision with another car in the summer fog. Gil's car rolled over, its windshield shattered, front end crumpled.

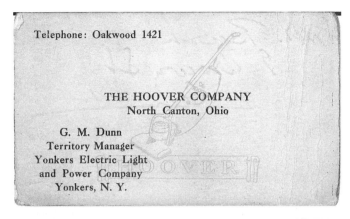

Gil managed an award-winning Hoover sales team.

Gil and two older women, social friends whom he was driving into the city as a favor, all were injured. One woman was thrown from the vehicle, and the other was pinned under the overturned car and suffered a broken arm and nose and abrasions. All this was reported in the *Putnam County Courier* read by everyone in Mahopac. Gil's car was unsalvageable, a complete loss. Was Gil not only injured himself but feeling guilty for all this damage? And, did he have to shield himself from his father's anger?

The very last photo in his album shows Gil asleep outdoors on an upholstered chair with head bandaged, and with a bandaged arm elevated on a pillow.

Roadster with rumble seat, 1938.

Smashed up.

Recuperating in Mahopac, August 1938.

The next year Gil and the two women sued the driver of the other vehicle, but I was unable to find the results of the suit. Even though this suggests that the accident may have been the other driver's fault, Gil still suffered bodily injury and time lost from work. This is another in a chain of misfortunes for Gil: color blindness, spinal meningitis, the Great Depression, and now a serious automobile accident.

Gil's convalescence this time sidelined him from work at Hoover in late summer of 1938 and probably into the early autumn. Did he fail to meet Hoover's aggressive sales targets? Was he moved to the top of the list of men to be let go because of his medical absence? By June 1939 Gil Dunn was again unemployed. Just when he was building another career, this time in management and sales, the opportunity disappeared, just as his Wall Street career had imploded. The second disappointment in his work life must have been piercing. His photo album stops abruptly here, its last fifteen black pages blank.

I discovered from the US Census and other sources that Gil went on to be unemployed all of 1940. I counted it all up. Gil, from the age of twenty-two to thirty, was out of work a total of five years in two stints. What does a bright, strong-bodied man do, emotionally, faced with this history?

Hoover Sales Office, 1939

The boss wants to see him.
He squares his shoulder,
touches the knot of his silk tie,
raps on the door.

Three minutes later he's out,
stands still as a bird
stricken by sound.
Not again. Why me?

What will he tell Pop
who's always had work,
good times and bad,
Pop who's always right.

I was service manager, for christsakes!
Twenty-nine and out of work
for who knows how long this time.
He sits on the park bench, staring.

My Father's Father: Martin Dunn

Because of my grandmother's comment about Martin's dark eye on Gil, I wanted to know more about Martin Dunn's life. Could I shed light on their father-son relationship? Going though Gil's album so many times, I came to notice just how many photos of his parents were mounted in those little black corners through the early 1930s when Gil worked on Wall Street. In the pages after, say, 1933 when Gil's unemployment began, there are no more photos of his parents, except one of his mother raking the lawn in Mahopac. Did this change in the album reflect a relational change in the home?

Rose and Martin Dunn, early 1930s.

Rose Dunn, fishing in high heels.

Martin and Rose,
Lake Cossayuna.

I had known my grandparents when they were elderly and had never given any thought to the arc of their lives. It dawned on me as I looked at their youthful photos that Rose and Martin Dunn were a prosperous and very stylish couple, brimming with health.

Paging through the album, I see them there, taking turns at target practice with a pistol, and there, pitching horseshoes. Rose wears slacks and holds a rod in one hand and a fish she's just caught with the other. In another photo she and Mart, as she called him, are in bathing suits, with a canoe atop their car. They are affectionate, just look at their hands.

I begin with Martin's country of origin. In 1857, at age eight, his father, Maurice, emigrated along with his father and brother from hardscrabble farm country in County Kildare. My immigrant great-grandfather Maurice could neither read nor write. He worked at a variety of jobs in Manhattan, including ostler (stableman), building superintendent, and foreman for street lighting; he married Mary Mullady, of pure Irish descent, and fathered nine children from 1884 to 1899.

By 1917 Martin's parents and five of his siblings had left Manhattan—in an early exodus to the suburbs—and settled on Long Island. Then, in 1927, his parents, in their seventies, along with the eldest son and the four daughters, all unmarried, drove across the country and settled for good in Long

Beach, California. I wish I could have listened to the seven of them deciding on this move! Was it for the climate, for jobs? Now no one remains to tell the story of the California Dunns. When I was a child we never heard about any family out West. How could we? We didn't even know that our grandpa came from a big family or that he was Irish. Where was the family feeling in my grandfather—that he could part forever with parents, a brother, and four sisters and not see them ever again? Or talk about them—as far as I knew. Was there a reason for the absence of family feeling?

My grandfather and three of his brothers stayed on the East Coast, and they all married, fathering a total of ten children. However, of the five Dunn siblings who moved to California, only two married, and only one had a child, one child. What was the dynamic inside the Maurice Dunn family that kept adult offspring so close to their aged parents? Once resettled in Long Beach, the family changed residence every single year until Maurice Dunn's death in 1933: Santa Fe Avenue, Baltic Avenue, Appleton Street, Elm Street, etc. This transience was an extension of Maurice's pattern of moving his entire family virtually each year in Manhattan and on Long Island, which I discovered by checking annual city directories. I wonder if in being the first to leave home, Martin Dunn was escaping from a family environment that was not healthy, that had marked him in some way? I can see a pattern—those many moves—but the causes, and other effects, remain unknowable.

Through US and New York State censuses I tracked my grandfather Martin's long career with New York Telephone: in 1910 bookkeeper, by 1920 "wire chief," and by 1925 engineer—at the age of forty. Martin Dunn had left school after third grade. This man learned on the job, and he climbed, through his effort and his wits, to the professional class by midlife.

Then there is Martin Dunn's New York National Guard service, beginning in 1906 at age twenty-one. In my online searches I happened on an article in a 1925 issue of the *New York National Guardsman Magazine*. How strange it was that as the PDF of this article slowly loaded on my laptop, I realized that my grandfather, then Lieutenant Dunn, was its author. He described how his unit set up telephone equipment at Camp Smith in Peekskill, north of New York City, during their summer training. Martin himself led the system design and managed the project. He writes that he asked General Dyer if he would like to speak to his brokerage firm in the city. In less than half a min-

Captain Martin Dunn, in riding gear, 1930s.

ute, to his delight, Dyer was connected and received the stock quotations of the day. A photo of Lieutenant Dunn with his commanding officer, General Dyer, accompanied the article.

Martin Dunn had connected with a very influential New York personage in George R. Dyer. Son of a former governor of Rhode Island, Dyer was a soldier, financier, and socialite. He would oversee major works projects in New York City, including the George Washington Bridge and the Holland and Lincoln Tunnels; at his death he was chairman of the New York and New Jersey Port Authority. As we've seen, it was through George Dyer—military man and stockbroker—that Martin Dunn installed his teenage son Gil in a job with prospects at Dyer's Wall Street brokerage firm.

By 1935 Martin Dunn was promoted to captain and named company commander of the 87th Brigade, an equestrian unit. Martin had a reputation for training his men to ride well.

Every Memorial Day in Manhattan he rode on horseback, often at the beginning of the parade near the grand marshal, I learned from the *New York*

Times. His expert horsemanship came about because his older cousin—with the same name, Martin, son of his father's brother Patrick—was a blacksmith by trade and by 1910 co-owned a stable on West 32nd Street in Manhattan. I imagine the two cousins exercising horses together. The propensity to horsemanship probably goes back to the family's origins in County Kildare, famous for horse breeding and racing, origins I was eventually able to trace back to the actual farmland in Lackagh (pronounced "Lacky"), from which the Dunns emigrated. (The four bachelor Dunn brothers living there today told me that at the time of the great emigrations, there was no work and no food, and that no one who left Lackagh ever wrote or came back.)

I was developing a new understanding of my grandfather Martin. Here was a man who forged his own way, pursuing the American dream. He was born into an illiterate immigrant laborer's large family in an era when there was intense discrimination against the Irish. NINA, "No Irish Need Apply," was a sign Martin saw posted in Manhattan windows. Through his career at New York Telephone and his National Guard service, Martin Dunn achieved material success, position, and respect. He dressed well and saw that his family was well provided for—his wife Rose and the children were always well turned out. He had the latest car, sent his family upstate on vacation every summer, and he was able to purchase the house in Mahopac in the midst of the Great Depression. Martin Dunn justifiably had the pride of a self-made man. He saw his son have advantages he never had. The many years Gil was out of work, living at home, unmarried, canoeing—this must have rankled Martin, the hardworking, ambitious father. Gil, for his part, was all too aware of his father's success and knew he didn't measure up, in his own eyes or his father's.

My grandfather loved work, its steadiness, its rewards—just like my brother, it turns out. After retiring from the New York Telephone Company after forty-five years, with a pension and Bell Telephone stock, my grandfather took a new job. He entered the civil service, and from 1952 to 1962 he commuted from Mahopac by car and ferry to Fort Jay, the military post on Governors Island, off lower Manhattan. His title was chief of the Telephone Engineering Branch, First US Army Signal Section. The *Civil Service Leader* newspaper headline announcing his final retirement at age seventy-seven was *Communications Expert Retires.* This makes me smile. Within our family, as I knew him, my grandfather was anything but an expert at communication.

In 1959 my grandparents celebrated their fiftieth wedding anniversary with dinner and dancing at the Tavern on the Green in Central Park with about twenty guests, all family, arranged by Gil's brother-in-law, Bill, who was well connected in the city. I have two vivid memories of this event, when I was thirteen. Starting my one and only waltz with my grandfather, who was stiff and uncomfortable holding me, I heard him say gruffly with annoyance: "Don't lead." Really, where was his kindness? And later at dinner my father got to his feet to make the evening's first toast. But he was not, as I expected, eloquent or witty. Instead he stumbled over his words, and what little he said was ordinary. I was astounded, then ashamed for him. This performance was out of keeping with my vision of him. I thought of him as a man who excelled. After all, wasn't his criticism of Mike, Mother, and me because we did not meet his expectations? I had made an idol of him, and now I had this glimpse that he was a mere man. I experienced this dissonance deeply, but my mind was unable to make any sense of it. It was like that old black-and-white puzzle: Is it a vase I see, or the profiles of two women? But the girl I was did not want that tongue-tied undistinguished man to be my father. And of course now I see my father's performance as, in part, a continuation of his difficult relationship with his father.

As his granddaughter, I knew Martin Dunn only as an old man who said "poil" for "pearl" and "goil" for "girl." He spoke that pure New Yawk-ese that in his time, I now know, was typical of the offspring of working-class Irish immigrants. On visits to us in New Hampshire he purchased cartons of whiskey at the state liquor store, his supply for months back home. He wrote the liquor off on his taxes as medicine. He and Grandma began their highballs right after noon struck. I never saw them drunk, but they drank a lot. They played bridge with my parents. Conversations always stayed on the light side. These were not introspective, political, or philosophical people. Father and son, Martin and Gil, never went for walks or drives together. Martin Dunn never accompanied my father to his business in Penacook, or fished with him on the Merrimack River.

Croquet, horseshoes, bridge—activity by the whole family or couples was the norm on those Dunn visits. Even when I was very young I was aware of something unusual. I would be sitting on the living room couch or waiting my turn with croquet mallet in hand, and I would overhear my father talking with his mother and sister. He laughed so easily, enjoying himself in a manner so different from the way he was with my mother and us children. His sister,

Muriel, who was pert and trim, teased him, and my grandmother enjoyed bantering with him. Both women were lighthearted and laughed a great deal. These were my father's template of Woman—and my mother turned out to be very different from them.

3: Years of Change: 1939–1941

The Encounter

In a photo dated 1940, Gil is quite the handsome man. It's summer, out-doors, and he's wearing two-tone wing-tip shoes, a crisp white shirt with sleeves are rolled short of the elbows, pants with a crease, silk tie. He looks, well, almost debonair, one foot resting on a bench. He's slim, yet mus-cled from canoeing and outdoor sports; he is one of those good-looking bald men, his remaining thin dark hair combed back. High cheekbones, thin lips, definite brows, expressive eyes.

Gil Dunn enjoyed, or played the role of enjoying, leisure after his Hoover job ended. Some young men in Duchess County, New York, near Mahopac, came from families of real wealth and did not work, or aspire to work. Was he friendly with one or two of President Roosevelt's sons, who grew up at Hyde Park in Duchess County? My aunt told me this. Did Gil somehow manage to carry off unemployment by appearing to be someone he was not? Did he say he was between jobs? Looking for the next good opportunity? Could he have had a false sense of what kind of work he should have, or his own version of false pride, no position seeming worthy of him? Could he have been truly at a loss, not knowing how to parlay his past experience, not actually trained in any profession or craft, so that he was at sea but always had to pretend he was not? As confident as he looks in this photograph, I suspect that he endured self-doubt, and bouts of low spirits, as the months of unemployment went on.

In his leisure Gil socialized with nurses from Hudson River State Hos-pital in Poughkeepsie. Sometime in the summer of 1939, one of the nurses he had dated, Leona Ward, asked him for a favor: he had free time—would he escort Mary Carmen, her fourteen-year-old sister, in a variety of outdoor

Gil, summer 1940.

activities? Big sister Leona, then thirty-four, from upstate New York, had taken Duchess County by storm—she was a hearty extrovert who loved flirting, making things happen, putting people together. She wasn't shy about asking for a favor.

Gil rowed the blue-eyed, buxom Mary Carmen on Lake Mahopac, took her to Crum Elbow Creek and to the Hudson River, gave her swimming lessons. He delivered her to family friends in a bohemian household in Carmel to spend a few days. Finally he brought the bobby-soxer, who by then was infatuated with him, back not to Leona but to her other older sister, which was how Gil Dunn met Dr. Gladys Ward.

Gil may have been struck right away by Gladys's thick brunette hair and strong features—which resembled those of Edna, his girlfriend in the early 1930s. Gil learned that Gladys Ward—she asked him to call her Glad or Glady—had been living and working on the hospital campus for three years, first as a medical resident, and now on staff as an assistant physician. She wore simple clothes, and in the style of the day she lacquered her fingernails bright red and wore lipstick to match. Unlike her vivacious and chatty sisters, Gladys was

Gladys Ward, late 1930s, photographed by her mother.

quiet, earnest, and serious. Perhaps Gil was intrigued that she was almost three years older than he and that she was dedicated to her medical career. Here was someone with the stability and sure career path that had eluded him: this may have been a strong unconscious attractant for him over time.

Was Gladys Ward so preoccupied with her work, the sixty-hour weeks, being on call weekends, that Gil's being unemployed just wasn't apparent to her? Maybe she saw him as "between positions." And it is very likely that this socially retiring woman was drawn to this good-looking available man who began to take some interest in her. Occasionally Gil and Glad played golf together and played bridge with friends; socializing was amiable, with cocktails and cigarettes. Was he flattered that this woman doctor was open to his social overtures? When he brought her to his family's home in Mahopac, did he think his stock would go up with his father? Did her achievement somehow add luster to him?

Strikingly, for a man who had been taking photos since he was sixteen, there is not one photograph of Glad taken by him from the time they met, through his military service—not until years later. And there is not one photograph of them together in 1939 or 1940—in fact, not until 1945. What could this mean? I discovered the beginning of an answer in the shoebox I'd kept in my closet.

This old shoebox of mine held hundreds of miscellaneous family photos. A stiff brown envelope with three-by-three-inch black-and-white film negatives was there as well, but I had always passed this envelope by. Now I peered at the negatives and suspected I had come upon photos of my father's from around 1938–39, when Gil's album stopped. I decided to have the negatives printed, and I was right. There was a shot, taken from inside a canoe, of Gil paddling and smoking a pipe. The next was of teenage Mary Carmen, holding that same pipe as she sat back, smiling, in the canoe. So, here was that fateful summer of 1939, days before Gil met Glad.

No prints from these negatives were in his album, or anywhere else. In addition to more photos of Mary Carmen in a bathing suit posing on a beach, Gil had taken photos of two attractive women, nearer his age, in bathing suits and of a well-dressed woman on a park bench, as well as photos of him and Kay skating. So, I believe that during the first years Gil knew Gladys Ward he was seeing other women and Glad played only a small part in his social life. My guess is that he threw away the prints of these negatives years later, when the relationship with Glad was a fact. And these negatives were forgotten. The absence of any photos of Gladys Ward points to the conclusion that Gil was not very involved with her. She was someone he knew, but he was taking other women out and photographing them.

As 1940 was rounding toward fall and winter Gilbert Dunn had been out of work over a year with no prospects in sight. He had traveled to Florida alone in May 1940 to go deep-sea fishing. Perhaps he was looking at Florida as a place he might relocate his life. That's conjecture, but if true it had led to no new direction. It seems to me, now that I am assembling the pieces of his story, that this man had no vision of himself and what he could do or be; he did not look into the future, let alone plan for one. It's as if he waited for life to happen to him. And just as the Depression had caught him in its gears, now the Army Air Forces and World War II were about to chew him up for another almost five years.

Becoming a Soldier

Europe was at war. In September 1940 the US Congress passed a bill requiring men between eighteen and sixty-five to register for the selective service, and Gil registered right away. Then he decided to enlist rather than be drafted.

Mitchel Field, February 1941.

His first choice was the navy, but his color blindness disqualified him. He was disappointed because, as a canoeist, swimmer, and fisherman, he had loved the water all his life. However, he ended up journeying significant amounts of time on oceans and seas during his service with the Army Air Forces, which inducted him in December 1940. Joining the military was viewed as a patriotic, brave act. By January 1941 Gil was in uniform, and he would not return to civilian clothes until July 1945.

Gil entered a new life. His world had comprised family, friends, the city, Mahopac, the Hudson River, speed boating, and his stylish clothes. On his mind, worries about not working and perhaps bravado about being unemployed. Now in January 1941, a month before his thirty-first birthday, he slept on a cot in a barracks at Mitchel Field on Long Island, ate in a mess hall, wore a uniform, learned military decorum, and met men from all over the country. This very structured life may have suited him after years of unstructured time out of work. His military superiors must have recognized talent and experience in him, because after only a month he was promoted from private to staff sergeant, a noncommissioned officer, usually leader of a squad. The promotion must have been heartening. Mitchel Field is not that

CHANUTE FIELD AND RANTOUL

Gil's postcard of Chanute Field and Training Center, Rantoul, Illinois.

far from Mahopac and Poughkeepsie, and Gil visited family and friends, including Glad, on leave.

In spring 1941 Gil was posted to Chanute Field in Rantoul, Illinois, an enormous technical training center where recruits learned aircraft maintenance. Returning to Chanute from a leave home in early July, Gil sent Glad a postcard: *Thanks for your letter, Glad. Received it just before lunch. So nice of you to be so considerate. Made the return trip on schedule, 22 hours, rain all the way. Tired? Yes, and car drunk too. Ever had the sensation?—Gil.* In late August, he wrote: *Hello Glad, Here is a panorama of Chanute, the home of Rantoul. Do you recall I mentioned some time ago that it was flat? Agreed? Just one week and a bit to go—get the clubs ready.—Gil.* So, on his leave Gil and Glad golfed together. The tone of these postcards was friendly, not romantic. They had known each other for two years. They were involved, but not very involved, and were not yet a couple.

By the fall of 1941, with his training in Illinois finished, Gil was assigned to the outfit he would spend the next three years with: the 59th Fighter Squadron, 33rd Fighter Group, of the Army Air Forces, then posted at an airfield in Baltimore. Curtiss P-40 Warhawks were manufactured in the nearby Glenn Martin plant, and the pilots and mechanics of the 59th trained on brand new P-40s. Each plane was a one-man, single-engine craft, armed with three machine guns in each wing; the pilot both flew the plane and fired the guns. Gil was leader of a squad of eight specialists repairing and maintaining aircraft—his title, crew chief. In jottings on the backs of photos he took of his barracks and mailed home, I hear his desire to connect with his father, captain in the National Guard; now they are both soldiers.

A Son Writes Home
February 1942

He sends home photos of his barracks
near Glenn Martin Field. His cot, one of forty,
his desk, a board. *"My den—all the conveniences,"*
he writes. *"Lunch cake and pop in evidence
on the desk."* He has arranged a still life
backlit by the sunny window: glass bottle
half full, cake and a pack of smokes
standing with three cigs sticking up like steps.
All staged for his father, I think, to say:
I am your good soldier.

"Do you recognize anything of yours, Dad?"
I peer at the sepia photo, drenched in sunlight.
Can he mean the binoculars? Or the lamp?
The men hang their clothes above the cots,
line up boots below. Potbelly stove.
"Here's a good shot," he writes. *"Picture taken at 10 a.m.
Saturday morning. Lack of soldiers is due
to the fact that they are working."*

> Except for him,
> taking photos, and one soldier he didn't notice,
> whose head peeks out from his blanket,
> eyes closed sleeping all these years.

In December 1941 the United States formally entered the war after Japan's bombing of Pearl Harbor. Gil knew the 59th would be headed overseas; the only question was when.

The Suitcase

Now, the suitcase comes into my father's story. This quite small suitcase from another era has honey-butter leather stitched with almost an inch of darker leather along the edges; the corners are reinforced with decorative metal. It bulges with Gil's correspondence to Glad—scores of wartime letters from overseas, hundreds of postcards including the early ones from Chanute, as well as documents, a journal kept on the homeward journey when it was impossible to mail letters. From these I was able to reconstruct Gil's whereabouts just before and during World War II. In beautiful lettering on the top surface of the suitcase my father penned the names of over one hundred places he fought in and traveled through, including Casablanca, Algiers, Tunis, Pantelleria, Sicily, Naples, Cairo, the Red Sea, Bombay, Karachi, Burma, the Himalayas, Chengtu.

Top surface of Gil's suitcase, 12 x 24 x 5 inches.

Why have I done such a lot of research on my father's Army Air Forces experience? Not only have I pored through the contents of this suitcase countless times, reading and rereading letters he wrote, but I've also researched his squadron's war experiences, online and in books. This took me from blog sites of veterans to books such as Paul Fussell's *Wartime* and Barbara Tuchman's *Stilwell and the American Experience in China*. I found two volumes, privately published, by a fighter pilot in his squadron, Lieutenant James R. Reed, with diary entries, candid photos, and remembrances by other members of his unit. I researched geography and battle formations. I wanted a sense of the lands where he served, his fellow soldiers, what his war experiences would likely have been, what he certainly saw and never wrote about or talked about. Why? To see if I could ferret out if his service in the military in three theaters of war contributed to transforming him from the sociable athlete, brokerage clerk, and sales manager of his earlier years to the solitary, judgmental, unhappy man I knew.

All along I've wanted to flesh him out, him as a living, feeling person, rather than live with a petrified ghost. Now in this journey with him overseas I would look at circumstances that may have affected him profoundly. And, importantly, here were more than thirty letters and more than fifty pages of a journal. What would they tell me about his view of the world, of his personality?

Gil's earliest overseas correspondence was a postcard I found in Glad's scrapbook. He mailed it in May 1942 from Port of Spain, Trinidad. This was puzzling—my father never mentioned having been in the Caribbean. I matched the postcard's date with a slip of paper I found in Gil's suitcase: it was a pass to go ashore from the aircraft carrier USS *Ranger*. The story of a special mission unfolded as I researched the *Ranger*'s history. His superiors assigned Gil away from the 59th to join a select group of crew chiefs who would ready sixty-eight aircraft destined to join the "Flying Tigers" fighting the Japanese in China.

The *Ranger* sailed from Rhode Island, south to the West Indies, then straight east across the Atlantic to West Africa. All aboard were informed that intense German submarine torpedoing meant there was only a fifty-fifty chance of surviving the mission. Gil and the other crew chiefs made sure the P-40s were flight ready, and from 120 miles off the Gold Coast the planes took off from the flight deck to Accra, Ghana, on the first leg of their journey across Africa, the Middle East, India, and over the Himalayas to join the Flying Tigers. On the return leg of this month-long journey Gil wrote his postcard to Glad. His selection from many hundreds of crew chiefs for this mission suggests that he had more than ordinary ability, ability that was apparent to his superior officers. In his postcard from Trinidad, Gil wrote Glad cheerfully about getting a tan. He'd had his first adventure.

4: The "Fighting Nomads" in Africa and Europe

Gil shipped out overseas again on October 17, 1942, and this time he would not return to the United States for more than two years. He boarded the USS *Anne Arundel* in Virginia as part of Operation Torch, the largest flotilla of men and materiel ever assembled—over thirty-five thousand men traveling in 102 ships over four thousand miles to their secret target: North Africa.

Operation Torch—Invasion of North Africa

Gil was now part of the Allied invasion of North Africa, which opened up a second front for the Atlantic theater. The Allies' intent was to give Germany two Atlantic fronts to contend with, to reduce the German pressure on Russia, and to block Hitler's access to oil in the Middle East. England, recuperating from the huge losses suffered in the retreat from Dunkirk in May 1940, was not prepared to do battle again in the European theater in 1942–43. And it was also feared that in 1942 even the US armed forces were not seasoned enough to launch a massive invasion in Europe. Thus with the invasion of North Africa Gil began what was to be two years overseas with the 59th, seeing battle first there, then in Italy, and in the China-Burma-India (CBI) theater. His fighter group, the 33rd, was one of the most traveled in World War II and has been dubbed the "Fighting Nomads."

Gil's troopship was one of eight ships in the Northern Attack Group that made amphibious landings near Port Lyautey, French Morocco, on November 8. I've read an account of another crew chief's experience at exactly this moment of the invasion, clambering down the netting on the side of the ship, and boarding an Army Air Forces crash boat (usually used to rescue downed pilots) and making the landing on the beach in heavy surf with the infantry, combat engineers, and armored units. The landing was conducted under fire from the Vichy French fortifications. Gil, like this other 59th crew chief, jumped into the water and waded to the beach, wearing an overcoat and carrying rifle, ammo, a full pack, and two toolboxes. Gil and other aircraft mechanics, the "air echelon," had their first mission: secure the nearby airfield for the arrival of P-40s set for two days later.

The airfield at Port Lyautey was severely damaged from shelling by the US Navy in its attempt to stop French planes from taking off. The ruts, shell craters, and rain-sodden ground would make landing extremely difficult for the American P-40s. Gil and others in the advance air echelon did their best to prepare the battered field. Nevertheless, seventeen planes were damaged on landing and had to be abandoned. Meanwhile, behind-the-scenes negotiations resulted in the French in Morocco quickly calling an end to resistance. The invasion was successful.

Each crew chief and crew were assigned to a pilot and plane. Gil Dunn and his men had been assigned to the P-40 of Lieutenant Frederick W. Mayo, Jr., twenty-seven, from Mississippi. From Gil's small suitcase I retrieved a pocket spiral notebook in which he recorded assignments. Each specialist focused on an area of Lieutenant Mayo's airplane: engine, propeller, electrics, instruments, landing gear and hydraulics, flight controls, and so on. Early in the Operation Torch campaign, Gil took responsibility with two others for the engine of "their" P-40.

Like all soldiers, Gil was proscribed from revealing any military details when he wrote home. Censorship was imperative. Every letter was read by an examiner and signed with name and rank. Only twice did a censor have to scissor out a place-name in Gil's letters. Gil never described actions or events he participated in or witnessed. This is typical of "war letters." Paul Fussell says in his book *Wartime* that to keep up morale on the home front, letters were composed "to hint as little as possible at the real, worrisome circumstance of the writer."

In his first letter to Glad from North Africa, Gil writes: *Hello "Darling," Surprised to learn that I jumped the country, or had you heard?* Never before had Gil used the word "darling" in writing to Glad. And it's in quotes, indicating tentativeness, as if he's not quite used to it or sure it's quite right. In their last encounter before he shipped out, Glad and Gil must have agreed to write each other exclusively, that they would be each other's gal and guy for the duration.

"IDLE GOSSIP SINKS SHIPS" *is the caution on the topmost envelope.*

It was a time of pitched emotions, leave-taking for war on Gil's part, and for Glad, at thirty-five years of age, maybe her last chance for a husband and family. Gil ends this first letter not with "Love" but with "As Ever."

By November 15, 1942, Gil was stationed in Casablanca, French Morocco, at Cazes Airdrome—the airport from which Ilsa Lund and Victor Laszlo depart for Lisbon at the end of the film *Casablanca*, though their airdrome was actually a studio backlot. The 59th was held in reserve at Cazes while other squadrons of their fighter group joined American and British troops at the battlefront farther east against the well-equipped and battle-experienced German forces.

However, in Casablanca the men of the 59th were dealt a blow. Their twenty-four surviving planes were to be given away—to reequip the Free French's Lafayette Escadrille squadron. The planes moved to the French side of the airfield, and the French circle was painted over the American star. The 59th's pilots trained the French pilots on the P-40s, and the American mechanics, including Gil Dunn, trained French crews. At the formal turnover, the 59th Squadron stood in line on the airfield and watched the Lafayette Escadrille take off in their P-40s. One member of the squadron wrote: "What a sad day for the 59th, in a hostile country without any planes. We were all very upset with losing P-40s that we had picked up new, and had taken such good care of, since we knew they would be our fighting machines."

It's a Windy Day in Africa . . .

The sun is shining brightly and I have taken cover in the cockpit of my plane, closing the canopy which admits the warm rays of the sun but shelters me from the gusty wind. Rolling hills and mountains meet the eye from all sides. Traffic on the road is heavy in both directions. There are planes, of course, with five-gallon tins for fuel everywhere.

On my right, about a mile away, is our camping ground. Beyond that is a small clustered nest of Arab dwellings, and strewn over the remaining area are isolated ones. On my left, and widely separated, are more isolated Arab enclosures. These hardly rate as homes for they consist of four stone walls about ten feet high, oblong, fifteen by thirty feet, and often roofless. They are made of fieldstone and mud, which is like our cement when dry. When there is a roof it's supported with tree spars and covered with stone or with salvaged junk, sometimes covered with earth or straw. The interiors are bare—no floors, no beds. During the day I have seen the Arab sprawl in the sun and sleep, but at night he huddles in a sitting crouch usually up against and on the leeward side of a stone wall and sleeps.

Off in the distance is a herd of possibly a thousand head. It's a mixed mass of cows, bulls, sheep and goats, tended by two Arabs. There go three Arabs galloping across the fields on horseback. The horseflesh here is of the best. Groups of camels are grazing in the hills. And I see a camel and a burro teamed together plowing a field—I don't know who leads who, but one is dependent on the other. Jeeps whiz about the airfield constantly. Roman ruins are here and there. But with all this expanse there are but a handful of trees. Only the toughest of grass in clumps and the hardiest of flowers and brush and cactus thrive in this region. The floor is a dusty green as far as the eye can see and the sky at present is a pale blue.

When I first read my father's letters and journal I was struck immediately by the quality of his prose. I remember thinking he possessed genuine talent. His writing showed a gift for narrative, lyricism, description, humor. I had no notion of this, so had never considered that my lifelong love of words and writing could have been "inherited" from him. Sadly, Gil found no reason to employ this talent later in life; perhaps he never realized he had this talent or that it could be developed. And as I knew him, he was a man of few words, mostly of criticism and commands.

Gil's mid-April letters to Glad find him commenting appreciatively on the scent of her letters: *The delicately perfumed stationery, pleasantly reminiscent of by-gone days, actually lessened the distance of many thousands of miles, to a point where your presence could almost be felt. . . . Keep it up, so I can whiff while I read, and dream while I sleep.* In later letters he called such fragrance "bait," as if he were a fish that might be hooked, or an animal, trapped. *Tabu arrived full strength, hmmmmm—good fishing.*

His letters described female bird behavior in great detail: *The sparrow, more gifted in song than ours are, chirps her merry piece in amazing variations while in non-progressive flight (due, I've imagined, to the shortage of trees). Her flight consists of a dart here, a loop there, a flutter, a soar, a pick-me-up, etc., which usually last from ten to twenty minutes, covering practically no ground at all, except height, and if I may repeat—still singing.* At times Gil called Glad "chickadee." His April 18th letter contained a long humorous tale, which I've included here, about his adventures with a duck. He named the duck Dona and said she was the sister of Dona _ _ _ _ _ _—I think those six blanks are for the letters in Gladys's name.

Dona, the Duck

Still North African Campaign, Sunday 9 pm, April 18th, 1943

Hello Lamb—

The chicken episodes have been a disappointing venture, so I've gone ducky. On two occasions I had fathered two promising looking hens. Set them up with beautiful ration boxes, lined with straw, and took great pains to face the coop in the opposite direction of the blowing winds each night before turning in. I fed 'em like queens, satisfied their thirsts, and in both instances beautiful friendships blossomed—but no eggs. So I liquidated my holdings by giving 'em back to the Arabs, and bought myself a duck.

Since this purchase was made away from the camp while on a special mission, due to the fact that I returned late at night I was forced to take the duck to bed with me, for fear of losing her. Her feet were tied, so she offered very little resistance. Which was indeed fortunate for her, for I was too tired to quibble since I had cuddled her under my arm for the past five hours, and none too gently at times, I'll admit. I could sense when we entered my abode that she was not the least bit ruffled. But I was—for my dugout, shared with a buddy, was none too large. Just big enough to stretch out in. So I placed her at the head of my bed, and there we slept (so I thought). I awoke at the crack of dawn and hearing a slight movement I turned around, and the sight frightened me momentarily. With the long neck sticking high in the air and the bill breathing in my face, I thought I was confronted with a cobra. Instinctively I withdrew, increasing the distance about two feet, and with better focus in the dim light, my lagging recollection told me, it was ducky. I must have frightened her too, and I doubt if she had slept much since she showed symptoms of being shy, not hitherto revealed. Later on I was to learn or assume the reason why. So jumping up, I tucked her under my arm (she's about two feet overall) and placed her on the roof, as a precaution against stray dogs (her legs still tied) and I went off to chow. Later on that day, inspection of my quarters revealed that ducky (Dona I named her, sister of _ _ _ _ _ _) had been conscientiously employed while I slept. For there at the head of my bed lay the fruit of her labors—an immense egg, estimated about the size of a pear with a shell the color of a sun-bleached pearl. True, it was broken and all over the place. Whether she or I did it, didn't matter for right there and then I knew we were going to be great pals.—That's where I was wrong. For that afternoon I moved out on special duty and I haven't seen Dona since. It's a sad story and a disappointing ending, Glad, I know, but somewhere, somehow, I'm sure that Dona and I shall meet again, and then this fowl story maybe continued.—Will Dona and Gil be reunited? Is Dona safe? Is she still putting out? These questions and many more may be answered if the African Campaign lasts that long, which is very doubtful.

As I reread Gil's letters I detect an element of "display" in them—he's showing off his ability to tell a story, describe a scene, deploy "fifty-cent" vocabulary, all executed in his artful handwriting. He wants to impress the well-educated recipient. An undertow of sexuality begins to run in the letters. *It is now about 10 pm, and the natives' dogs, off in the distance, are again, going at it hot and heavy. . . . You have acquired the most interesting and jovial bedroom penmanship it has ever been my pleasure to receive . . . and in closing may I suggest that you don't think too harshly of the Atlantic City Wolves. There is a much more vicious breed.* [signed] *Sicilian Wolf.* While his letters are charming, and sometimes threaded with a gentlemanly eroticism, what I do not see in Gil's letters are serious feelings, longings, memories, a curiosity about Glad, or substantive ideas—instead they present a decorative surface.

Meanwhile, the 59th had been resupplied with new planes in March 1943, the pilots were again flying missions, and the crews were kept on alert. In April the pilot whose plane Gil had maintained was shot down. The 59th Squadron never saw Lieutenant Mayo again. The losses mounted, took their emotional toll. (Lt. Frederick W. Mayo, Jr., I found out, through online research, was taken prisoner by the Germans and spent the rest of the war in Stalag 7A in Bavaria before liberation from the camp in 1945.) Throughout spring Gil's outfit ranged all over Tunisia at various airfields. *We have moved again. . . . I become fondly attached to each and every location, and do all within my means to make it habitable, with a smattering of comfort. . . . I have treasured possessions, mostly memories, scattered all over Africa.* But in fact Gil enjoyed the constant movement and boasted about flying more than a thousand miles over North Africa.

During spring 1943 in the midst of traveling all over Tunisia, Gil was preparing an application to be commissioned as a second lieutenant. Perhaps a superior had encouraged him to apply. His age—he was now thirty-three—may have motivated Gil; he may have felt he should be farther along in rank and responsibility. He was acutely aware that the other crew chiefs were in their twenties; the pilots, some in their early twenties, ranked as second lieutenant officers or higher. Gil never mentioned applying for a commission to Glad, nor did he ever express in any writing I have seen a desire to advance in the Army Air Forces.

In the application Gil stated that he was a graduate of high school. In fact, he attended one year. He stated that he worked at Hoover up until he volunteered for service. In fact he was unemployed for a year and a half before enlisting. He created a better record for himself—a record I am sure he wished he had. He acquired letters of recommendations from his superiors, sat for a photograph, and underwent a physical: weight 161 pounds, height 5 feet 10 and a half inches, blood pressure 118/80, IQ 137. His own comment was solicited to help ascertain "your best field of usefulness." He wrote: *I feel confident that the experience gained in the passed* [sic] *two years plus my civilian background as organization and production manager might be applied more advantagesly* [sic] *to the interest of the government. I am also a firm believer that I have been endowed with a fair amount of good common sense.* Gil sent off the paperwork and learned that he would be interviewed before a military panel in June, and that the panel's decision would be handed down by midsummer.

On May 11, 1943, Gil posted Glad a V-mail: *It was a tough fight, but now the job is done—here.* The headlines in the United States read: *Axis Smashed in Africa.* Gil marched down the broad palm-lined avenue through Tunis with thousands of Allied troops in the first Allied victory celebration of World War II. Then on June 10, while the Allies began their air assault on the Italian fortress island of Pantelleria, forty miles from Cap Bon in Tunisia, Gil had flown west to Algiers to appear before the panel considering his application for a commission.

Official photograph accompanying Gil's application for a commission as an officer, North Africa, spring 1943.

Four officers sat at a table: a colonel, two majors, and a second lieutenant. They interviewed Gil, and then dismissed him. They had read the recommendations of Gil's superiors:

". . . for his personality, ambition and clean cut manner."

". . . a credit to the engineering department . . . shows the high ideals necessary in an officer."

". . . a superior soldier. His habits, character and morals are excellent; his intelligence above average."

"He has demonstrated unusual intelligence and ability in his work and in the everyday affairs of the Squadron. His courtesy and exceptional military bearing are such as to recommend him to anyone. As an officer he will be a distinct credit to the service."

"He has those attributes of character and leadership which are indicative of a good potential officer. I take great pleasure in recommending him."

These recommendations were positive, to be sure, but in no way specific, recounting no incidents or examples of leadership. Gil's own statement, with its two spelling mistakes, did not make a strong case. However, I expect Gil was hopeful. The panel's decision would come within thirty days.

Pantelleria, Sicily, and the Italian Campaign

Gil waited for the panel's decision first on the tiny island of Pantelleria, which had been conquered after very heavy bombing, then in Sicily after a short conflict with the German Luftwaffe.

In the beautiful seaside town of Licata in Sicily Gil received the rejection of his application. "The applicant lacks the general military knowledge and

Licata - Corso V. Emanuele Superiore

Licata, Sicily: One of hundreds of postcards Gil mailed Glad.

experience to warrant a direct appointment as an officer." Even though the letter stated that this rejection would have no bearing on any future application, Gil did not apply again. I can imagine another man might apply again in a half year, or a year later. Gil kept the bulky paperwork (in triplicate) in a hand-sewn canvas envelope with snap, and it was in the leather suitcase when I opened it.

If Gil had hoped to make a career in the Army Air Forces, that hope was dashed. Even if he didn't want to make the military his career, I am sure he was humiliated by the rejection. His superior officers would know the commission did not come through. He must have swallowed this latest in a string of life disappointments with some shame. His father was a captain in the New York National Guard, his father's younger brother, Ray Dunn, had forged a military career and was a brigadier general in the Army Air Forces, and his brother-in-law, Bill, was an Army captain in the European theater. Gil was to remain a staff sergeant to the end of his service. This was a high noncommissioned rank, and he had achieved it early. Did it occur to him that the panel might consider his leadership of a crew as essential to upcoming campaigns and that promotion might rob them of a needed leader at the squad level? I doubt it: this was a "failure"—like his two lost jobs, another blow to his sense of self.

Italian Campaign

By mid-August 1943 the German and Italian forces had evacuated from Sicily, and the American GIs actually had free time to sightsee. Gil traveled to the active volcano Mount Etna in northeastern Sicily and mailed Glad US pennies embedded in small crusty chunks of black Etna lava. These were displayed in a bookcase in our house when I was growing up. His last station in Sicily was in Milazzo on the northern coast, sited to provide air support for the invasion of the mainland of Italy.

Launched September 3, the Allied invasion aimed to drive out the occupying German forces. Gil had now participated in three invasions: North Africa, Sicily, Italy. The 59th pilots supported ground forces as they advanced and attacked enemy aircraft on the air and ground; for Gil and the ground crews, maintaining the planes, mission after mission, was intense work.

By the end of December the activity of the 59th diminished, and Gil took in sights near Naples, including Capri's famous Blue Grotto and Mount Vesuvius and the ruins of Pompeii. My father saw so many remarkable sights—

these and many more to come—yet he never shared memories of them with my brother and me. We did not hear about Etna erupting or the luminous light in the Blue Grotto; in fact, you would never have known that Gil Dunn had traveled far and seen so much—it was as if these experiences were put away on a shelf in a dark closet that never again saw the light of day. How I would have loved to hear him describe Africa, Sicily, Italy . . .

In one of the leather wallets in my father's suitcase I found photographs of Glad taken in the late fall of 1943. They probably reached Gil sometime that winter in Italy. Glad is sitting on the fender of her car—she was in Ogdensburg in Upstate New York visiting her mother, at Thanksgiving. How many times did Gil take these photos out to look at them as he wrote to her?

In his January 4, 1944, letter from Italy to Glad, he wrote: *Well, well, LaGuerre—what a revelation to find myself enwrapped in one and courting another.* Glad had written him that LaGuerre was the original French family name of her father, whose parents were French Canadian; *la guerre* translates to the English *war* and was eased over to the more acceptable English name Ward. Here, finally, is Gil's outright statement that he is courting Glad. His overseas correspondence is his courtship, over continents, over years.

Glad, 1943, age thirty-six.

5: On to China

On February 22, 1944, on the eve of his thirty-fourth birthday, Gil boarded ship and sailed the Mediterranean from Italy to Port Said on the Suez Peninsula. After fifteen months in North Africa, Sicily, and Italy, flying a total of 4,048 combat sorties, Gil's 59th Fighter Squadron had ceased operations in the European theater and departed the heel of Italy, newly assigned to the CBI theater—China, Burma, India. Gil was shipping out to India where new aircraft awaited the 59th.

By the 29th of February Gil was stationed for a few days at Camp Huckstep, an American Army camp fifteen miles outside Cairo. What did he experience, seeing the Pyramids of Giza, the Sphinx, those remarkable feats of engineering, monuments of antiquity and mystery? He sent Glad several postcards of these sites but with only the briefest of notes.

The Pyramids
for my son

I put this picture on your bureau:
three soldiers on camels in front of the Pyramids,
your handsome grandfather is thirty-four, it's *Cairo,*
1944 in his florid script on the photo's edge.
In the middle of his long hitch in World War II—
Sicily, North Africa, India, Burma, China—
atop a camel he's smiling at us.
My father died twenty years before you were born.
He never really knew me. Why did I always
read three books at once? Why would I want

to go to college? I thought I knew him by heart.
Alone working at his woodshop,
mixing a highball at the kitchen counter,
finding fault with your Uncle Mike,
watching TV every night, eating lunch
at his desk, alone, alone. How proud I was
when he asked me to look at the name
he invented for his business. How proud I was
at five when I saw my drawing on the shop wall:
To Daddy from his gril Sharon. You, my boy,
have been happier in nine years, than he ever was
as I knew him. The smile in this photograph
so rare I wanted it here for you.

Aboard the English ship *Stratheden*, Gil sailed the Red Sea, then the Arabian
Sea, and finally reached the Indian subcontinent. On April I he left Bombay
by train and after five days' travel across India he reached Calcutta on the Bay
of Bengal. At the airfield there his unit trained on new aircraft.

In Egypt:
Gil, on right,
March 4, 1944.

I never knew these simple facts, that my father sailed the Red Sea or crossed the width of India by train . . . Perhaps the experiences and sights of travel were so bound up with war and its stresses for Gil that they could not be separated out to be talked about, let alone to be relished.

In early June Gil Dunn was on the final leg of his journey to China. He flew from Calcutta to the northeastern Indian province of Assam, from which the 59th set off for China over the Himalayan Mountains—flying "the Hump." Large daily transport planes flew among the eighteen-thousand-foot peaks in the eastern Himalayas to Yunnan airfield in China. Violent turbulence, high winds, ice, and other bad weather conditions were the norm. There were no reliable flight charts, no radio navigation aids, and scant weather information. By 1942 the Japanese had control over the Burma Road, the only land route connecting India to China. Flying "the Hump" was the only way that armaments, supplies, and personnel could get from India to China to support the war effort against the Japanese, who were well entrenched in China, especially in the north.

Confusion and stalemating characterized US involvement in China, and this atmosphere filtered down to soldiers like Gil Dunn. America's mission there was to reform the huge Chinese army, provide equipment and training to the Chinese, and to fight the Japanese in Asia. Yet General Joseph Stilwell had quickly realized that China's leader Chiang Kai-shek was more interested in combating Mao Zedong and the Communist forces than in fighting the Japanese.

Gil's unit was stationed near airfield A6, Fungwanshan, China. Gil wrote Glad his first impressions of China—from the air and when he landed. I've included an excerpt from May 1944, showing again Gil's gift for observation and expression that unsettled me. Why unsettled? Because I wondered what happened to the sensibility that wrote this. Wouldn't someone who could perceive and write in this way be a person sensitive to other people?

China, from the Air

From the air the country is one of the most beautiful spectacles that I have ever seen. The landscape is patterned into sweeping graceful curves of individualistic irrigated vegetation. Rice paddy fields in their water-laden beds appear translucent, which

*mirror-like, reflect the glow of the sky. Most farmland back in the States and the world
over is cultivated along angular lines, but not so in China. Every field and bed is tilled
and planned around the irrigation benefits the property affords. So that the land pattern
seen from the air is strikingly different and has the design of gracefully coordinated
curves which, when viewed as a composite, puts one in mind of a gigantic window of
stained glass that might in miniature adorn the most elaborate cathedral.*

*That was at least my impression as I flew through the clouds, but when the wheels
of our plane touched the ground and from then on in, I can say that we really have been
brought down to earth.*

*After two and a half months here, I have nothing but pity for the millions of hu-
manity that are born into poverty and burn themselves out at backbreaking labors till
they die, without benefit of reward other than a half-filled bowl of rice and a sip of tea.
In spite of their antiquated ways of life, which make their daily existence a solid day of
sometimes excruciating toil, they seem to be complacent and quick to laugh.*

*The white man here in China is considered a strange and interesting creature. I
stopped at a little shop display on the street to purchase a penknife. There was nothing
unusual in my behavior as far as I could see but by the time I had made my selection
and paid the merchant, at least a hundred Chinese had gathered about to witness the
transaction.*

Compared to the other theaters of war that the 59th had fought in, fewer
missions were flown in China, and boredom set in. In addition, every man
could see that scant supplies were directed to China—and those were often
commandeered for black market profiteering by both Chinese and Americans.
The Army Air Forces was short on war materiel and it was also experiencing
a severe shortage of food.

Gil wrote Glad in the summer of 1944: *We haven't been paid for three months,
but even that is of little importance since one couldn't buy an iced drink if he had a thousand
dollars. . . .* In another letter: *China is bearing down on the nervous system these days. It
has settled down to a repetitious state, as do all locations. The food situation is a little rough.
The same thing day in and day out till cigarettes take highest billing on the daily menu. . . . If
it wasn't for the hen fruit, god bless the chicken, the food situation would be really serious. If
I get 'em three times a day I'm satisfied. It isn't good that way, I know, but it's either that or
nothing and the latter leaves me with that empty feeling which is a sad alternative.* Eggs often
were the only food available to the soldiers. Gil had lost about twenty pounds
by this time.

⌇

In September 1944 the Army Air Forces transferred Gil out of the 59th Fighter Squadron. Gil received travel orders to ship to the United States— once he reached home on the East Coast he would have a twenty-one-day furlough before leaving for his next post. Why did Gil not stay with the 59th, as they went on to their next missions, including opening the Burma Road? Why was he singled out to return to the States? Perhaps it was his turn to "rotate" home. However, the more likely answer is that his superior officers noticed a change in his attitude and/or behavior. He had lost a great deal of weight. Was his performance as crew chief suffering because he was literally starving? Was he unable to manage his crew of eight men? Were there incidents?

On October 17, 1944, his homeward journey by air and water began. In pencil on the back of one of Glad's envelopes he noted his departure from China for India:

Wed Oct 18 3:15 p.m. shipped out in a C47 for Agra. Me—I'm just thinking of home— Glad, Mom, Pop, Muriel, Butch, Mahopac, old times and new ones to come.

This last jotting is one of only two expressions about the future that I have found in all of Gil's writings. It has Glad's name first, Glad the woman he had been writing to ever since he entered the military, the woman on his mind in the cockpit of a plane parked on the African desert, in his foxhole, in a tent, in an underground hangar. The idea of Glad was his companion everywhere he went. She was the woman of his dreams—and that is exactly it: she was a dream he conjured—based on his desire, his experiences with women in his past. The gap between the dream and reality was to hit both of them eventually.

In India for two weeks waiting to ship home, Gil started a journal in pencil on large single sheets of thin paper—he figured that he would arrive home before his letters at this point, so he would write a journal. He had time for sightseeing, recording one remarkable sight only tersely: *Visited Taj Mahal. Beautiful.* In October 1944 he wrote at length, though, about an experience on the bank of a tributary of the Ganges River, where he went to see the funeral pyres, the burning ghats. He witnessed the water burial of a young woman and described it in detail. How much did Gil see of death and wounds during the three invasions he participated in, on the airfields, in foxholes, that may have been as emotionally devastating as this ritual in the river?

The Burning Ghats

Hired a cart and visited the burning ghats, burial place of this sector. Nothing on the fire, many smoldering heaps of ashes. It was late in the day, about 4 p.m. The site is located on the banks of a dirty, brown, swiftly moving river. The ashes are usually thrown into the stream after cremation. It cost from 10 to 20 rupees for this service, American equivalent $3–$6. Those that cannot afford this expense are cast into the river intact and quickly consumed by the mammoth turtles, which attack immediately. Some cults due to their religious beliefs always cast their dead into the waters.

We were about to depart when an open drawn two-wheel cart with six men and their cargo, a solitary figure draped with beautiful cloth cover, drove into sight. So we lingered, bent on seeing what we came to witness. The body was borne, fully draped, to the bank of the river. There was practically no ceremony and the husband, who was one of the six, lifted the covering slightly exposing the slender brown arm of a woman, ringed with bracelets. He slipped off only one, a thick bright silver ringlet, the largest of them all and recovered the arm. He then stuck his hands under the covering at the head and removed the earrings. This done, the body was lowered into the fast moving waters and pushed off the thatch-made carrier, as the covering was withdrawn.

For a brief second the nude body of a pretty young Indian woman, as supple as she was in life, for death must have occurred only a short time before, was completely revealed. Her body blended with the water as she slipped out of sight, that is, all but her breasts, which were beautifully fresh, the tips of her slender shoulders and her lovely face. The current moved her slowly down the stream, all but ten feet offshore, and it was less than thirty seconds when her body suddenly jerked violently. The turtles were at work. She floated calmly for a few seconds more and shook visibly once again, then several times more as her head rolled from side to side violently. Then the body was drawn under the surface. It rose a few seconds later a little further downstream, still pitifully beautiful and from all appearances unmarred. Meantime the waters about her were turbulent and became increasingly so as more of these monstrous turtles swarmed about and occasionally broke the surface of the water. The body swayed and pitched as it was being wracked below the surface. As I left, one of the hard-shelled giants broke the water at the girl's side and clawed astride the girl's chest and they submerged as one.

6: Back to the USA

From Gil's Notes:

Oct 24–30 1944. Still waiting for orders to board ship. . . . Received our physical this morning, the 30th—any time now. Couldn't sleep last night . . . too restless—thoughts leaping here and there—all mostly about the States as I remember it—the land of the free. Regimentation is Hell.

Nov 2nd. Good news—boarded train en route to the boat at 10 a.m. On boat—a sweet job—USS General Anderson riding at anchor in Bombay at 1 p.m.

Nov 3rd. No steam up yet, still loading passengers—British, Persians, Indians, Chinese and us.

Staff Sergeant Gilbert Dunn sailed from Bombay on November 3, 1944, on a troop transport ship built during the war and designed for point-to-point transfer of large numbers of troops, dockside to dockside. This class of ship didn't have the capacity to assure survival of some fifty-five hundred passengers and crew in case of sinking, though I doubt the passengers knew this at the time. From Bombay Gil sailed to Australia and finally reached San Diego—over a month at sea, covering about fifteen thousand miles. A small oil painting of the USS *Anderson* always hung on the wall between Gil's twin bed and his wife's.

Gil arrived in San Diego on December 9, and four days later he boarded a crowded troop train for the East Coast, arriving in New York on December 18, 1944, exactly four years from his induction into the military. His twenty-one-day furlough was starting and would change his life.

At this point I feel compelled to look closely at the "romance" of Gilbert Dunn and Gladys Ward. What was its timeline, what was its reality? I asked my mother's younger sister, Mary Carmen, how well Glad knew Gil when he joined the military in December 1940, a year and a half after they met in the summer of 1939. She told me, "They were social acquaintances. Your mother really was lonely. She had no close relationships, she was working all the time." And in the following two years, when Staff Sergeant Dunn was in training in the United States, he mailed Glad those few postcards that had not a whiff of romance. *Dear Glad . . . More Later, Gil* were the hail and farewell of these cards before Gil went overseas.

Mary Carmen painted a picture for me of the everyday life of women like her and my mother during the war years: "There were no men! All the good men, the eligible men, were in the armed services." And I know this fact about my mother: she loved children and she wanted to be a mother, she wanted family life. Her ideal was not to be the woman wedded to a career.

In fall 1942 on leave in Mahopac, Gil knew he was shipping overseas soon. Who knew how long this war would go on, and if he would return? Glad and Gil, who had met more than three years earlier, agreed they would write each other, that they would be "there" for each other. Gil was perhaps the only attractive single man of Glad's acquaintance—not as strange as it sounds, given the long hours Glad worked at the hospital, among almost entirely married male colleagues, and how socially retiring she was. I can imagine Glad, impelled by her desire for a deeper relation that could lead to marriage, took the initiative. Wasn't Gil her last best chance? Gil, for his part, perhaps was flattered that this educated woman who obviously liked him was seeking him out. It was only letters, after all.

Despite Gil's first letter to Glad from North Africa in November 1942, in which he greeted her *Hello "Darling"* with those hesitant quotation marks, over time he progressed to salutations affectionate, even flowery: *Hello Lamb, Hello Sweet, Hello Darling* (no quotation marks), *Dear Streamlined Lady of Jet, Hello Baby.* The closing words of his letters are equally tender: *Bon Soir Ma Cherie, G'Night Ma-Lady, Good Night Darling, Nacht Leibling, Night Darlin'.* In the intensity of these greetings and endings I see Gil winding himself up, stoking his imagination and his fantasy.

Setting aside the Christmas 1942 note to Gil, the three wartime letters of Glad's that survive are all dated September 1944. Gil received them in China,

Glad and Gil's kid sister, Muriel, waiting for their men serving overseas, 1943.

when he knew he would be returning to the States and Glad did not know that yet. Her greeting was always *Hello Darling*, and she closed with *All My Love, Gladdy*. The tone of her letters was conversational, as if she were in the same room as Gil, telling him about her day, how she was going to frame a silk weaving he sent her, what a dinner cost at the restaurant down the road.

The longer Gil and Glad were apart, the more their imaginations must have created an ideal partner to yearn for, in the midst of—for him—soldiering, being strafed, seeing pilots crash, enduring ennui, rationing of water and food, and also the disappointment of his failed application to be an officer. And Glad, wanting her own family life, idealized him amid long hours that included psychotherapy, teaching, and supervising other therapies including electroshock and insulin.

On August 15, 1944, from China, Gil wrote, *Hello, Pet!* and farther down on this first of six sheets of US Army Air Forces stationery with, in the lower right corner, a cartoon of a turbaned snake charmer piping two snakes out of a basket: *Of course I have been anxiously awaiting your answer to my letter of July 13th.* But his July 13th letter is missing! *It takes a Philadelphia lawyer to figure out where one stands these days in the affaire du coeur. . . .* "Is you is or is you ain't" *is not a foolish question,* he continues,—*that's what I'm waiting to hear.*

"Is You Is or Is You Ain't My Baby," sung by Louis Jordan, was at the top of the US hit parade in late July through August 1944 and reached China on Armed Services Radio. The song wonders if maybe "my baby's" found somebody new or is "my baby" still "my baby" true? Glad's letter in reply is also missing, but the answer could only have been yes, affirming they were sweethearts. I infer this because the remainder of Gil's overseas correspondence does not let up with flowery beginnings and endings such as his October 6, 1944, *Hello Pardner* and *'Night, Sweet! Love, Gil.*

Reading his letters, I am surprised at how little, virtually nothing, really, Gil asked Glad about her work, how she found his parents (because photos show she visited them), how Mary Carmen, now a student at the Pratt Institute, was faring. Maybe Glad's missing letters provided ample news with no prompting. Gil's letters describe his tent, the landscape, sometimes an entire letter is about an escapade. In one he took six pages to narrate the drama of a flash flood that inundated the foxholes of his sleeping squadron in North Africa. In another he described sleeplessness in Sicily, tossing and turning, then up and happening upon a poker game, to bed hours later—only to be bitten all over by a centipede that had meanwhile hidden in his sleeping bag. And there's that tale of Dona the Duck in Italy.

I brood on what is missing in Gil's letters. He does not actually relate to Glad as a person, there are no real questions about her state of mind, what life is like for her. Expressions of missing her, or recollecting her or any time they shared, are rare. This is a huge vacancy—and I believe that Gladys Ward did not perceive it.

On October 20, 1944, Gil mailed Glad a packet of six postcards. His handwriting is uncharacteristically huge—he is excited, thrilled, announcing that he is coming home and says this will be his last correspondence, he'll call collect once he's reached the States.

∿

afraid something will happen to it. But it won't! You are the most beautiful thing that ever happened to me and that anything could happen to this lovely thing is unbelievable. I love you completely, darling—and feel sure that your love for me is equally sincere which makes things perfect. . . . I was so unbelievably tongue-tied when it came time to say good-bye. I was so afraid of bursting into tears and disgracing you—or undermining your morale that I said nothing. Just believe me when I say that nothing could have been lovelier than our last two weeks.

I wince because I read between the lines, between the words. Glad wrote that she was "dreadfully afraid" and I *know* she was afraid: the marriage she wanted so very much was on unsure ground, and now the husband she barely knew was gone. And I wonder what Gil felt when he read this letter—perhaps relief that he was away from her, distancing himself from the difficulties, the shame, of the honeymoon.

Where did Gil go on January 19? He was not posted to nearby Mitchel Field on Long Island as they expected. Instead he received orders to proceed to the Army Air Forces Convalescent Hospital at Bowman Field, Louisville, Kentucky, where he stayed until late May. Did Gil know he was going to a hospital and did he hide that fact from Glad, or was it a surprise to both of them?

Mother told me that my father went to Bowman for knee surgery, and all my life that is what I believed. However, recently as I learned about my father's problematic work history and stresses experienced overseas in his service during the war, and as I reflected on his father's relation to him, the thought came to me that he was manifesting psychological symptoms in China that sent him to Bowman. That could explain why he was singled out from his squadron to return to the States. I pushed that thought away time and again. I applied for a copy of his military medical records but was informed they had burned in a records fire in St. Louis, so I had no facts to go on.

However, I had to squarely face his time in Bowman. Why would his wife, a medical doctor, expect him to be posted to an airfield in Long Island if he had a knee requiring surgery? And I asked my brother: Do you remember any scars on either of Dad's knees? We saw him in bathing trunks in summer and we would have noticed. No, neither of us recalled a scar. Did my mother fabricate the knee story to "cover" for my father to us children? His having been in Kentucky was, oddly, a fact that we knew, and it needed to have a reason.

I learned that by 1944 the Army Air Forces had established twelve convalescent hospitals for fliers and other AAF soldiers who had seen combat.

These hospitals provided psychiatric services for men who suffered from what we began to call, in the 1970s, post-traumatic stress disorder (PTSD), and was then called operational or battle fatigue. Psychiatrists evaluated patients, and the men participated in group counseling sessions and occupational therapy—such as woodworking and engine repair or classes in starting a small business.

In 1946 film director John Huston under commission from the US Army made a very moving hour-long unstaged documentary, *Let There Be Light*, about a veterans hospital like Bowman. *The soldiers we see on screen*, the narrator intones, *are casualties of the spirit, men who are emotionally damaged and troubled in the mind. Born and bred in peace, educated to hate war, they were overnight plunged into sudden and terrible situations. Every man has his breaking point, and in the fulfillment of their duties as soldiers, they were forced beyond the limit of human endurance.* (The documentary revealed so clearly the mental damage suffered by soldiers that the US Army refused to issue it, claiming it would undermine military morale. It was finally released in the 1980s.) Gil had struggled with unemployment, with health, with his father's disdain. Now the weight of two years overseas at war had tipped the balance.

Gil was wrestling with his demons. Within a month of his arrival at the convalescent hospital Gil wrote to Glad stating that their marriage was a mistake and he wanted to end it. I never read the letter he sent her, but I once read the letter Glad wrote to him in reply, which beseeched him to realize how much the war had affected him, as well as his time convalescing in Kentucky; she said her love was unshakable, strong enough for both of them. Yes, with one of my mother's hairpins I picked the half-inch key lock in the small closet in my father's basement workshop in New Hampshire. I was eleven. How early I began the search for the secrets of my parents! That letter too is gone now. I do remember my discomfort, almost disbelief, when I read it.

In my father's suitcase there is no Army paperwork regarding the Bowman hospital, only a patient's meal punch card and a pass to travel no more than sixty miles from Louisville. A single photo dated May 1, 1945, shows fourteen soldiers posing outside a barracks. The one fellow in full uniform sits in front on a duffel bag—the photo memorializes his departure. Gil in the back is peering over someone, and I can tell he is smiling for the camera. The average stay in AAF convalescent hospitals was six to eight weeks. Gil Dunn's stay was double that—over sixteen weeks.

Sometimes I think Gil Dunn's stay at Bowman is central to my understanding everything that happened later. A psychiatric convalescence must have changed how he saw himself, and how Glad thought about her new husband. Gil would have had to allow into his consciousness, maybe for the first time in his life, that he had problems. Depression? Personality disorder? Where once I interpreted Gil's letter about divorce as an expression of his distaste of Glad, of marriage, can it be read another way? Maybe he was offering Glad a way out? Was he saying, I know you didn't sign up for being married to a "mental case"? And he would want to escape marriage altogether if sex seemed an insurmountable obstacle.

I believe Gil did not realize the loyalty, sympathy, perseverance, and practicality that were natural and deep in the woman he had married. Glad took her marriage vows seriously. She had a large heart. She was dogged in the belief that her efforts could help him and make the marriage work. She was thirty-eight years old, concerned that her time to bear children was running out. She offered him what a psychiatrist in the Huston film said was necessary to begin to heal—a relationship with someone who relieves the soldier's isolation, who affirms self-worth. The question in my mind all these years later is: was Gil's personality receptive to these true offerings?

❧

The happiest photo of Gil and Glad, with Glad's sister Mary Carmen and step-father Will Shaffer, August 1945.

The weekly newspaper covering Mahopac, New York, ran a social note that Staff Sergeant and Mrs. Dunn visited his parents on May 31, soon after he left Kentucky. Glad had convinced Gil to give the marriage a chance. By mid-July Gilbert Dunn was honorably discharged from the Army Air Forces and returned to civilian life, civilian clothes. That summer they visited Glad's mother in Ogdensburg, who took a photograph of Glad and Gil with true smiles on their faces . . . they are both looking at the twenty-year-old Mary Carmen. This is the only time I have seen my father wearing a wedding band.

Another artifact to be interpreted: a photo of Glad sitting in a lawn chair in her mother's backyard taken the summer of 1944, *before* Gil shipped home. A small leather picture folder in his suitcase held this one photo. On its back Gil wrote their wedding date and a second date with meaning known only to him: *Jan 4th 1945 Aug 29th, 1945.* For a long while I had imagined the second date meant the end of any illusion of marriage for him, but now I entertain alternative conjectures. Perhaps after almost nine months of doubt he recommits to the marriage? Or, perhaps August 29 is the date the marriage was consummated?

My revised thoughts about the meaning of the second date seem to best fit the spirit I see in the couple in the earlier photo: their genuine smiles, his

Gil wrote two dates on the back of this photo of Glad

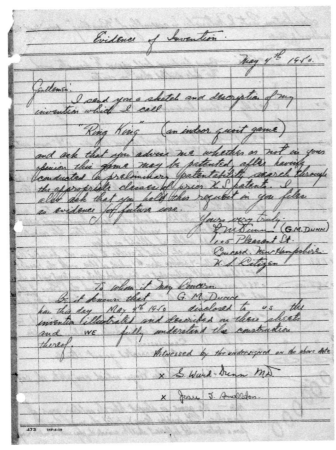

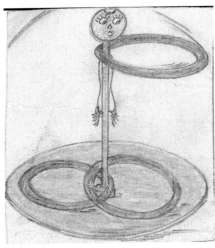

"Evidence of Invention" of a game
Gil considered patenting, 1950

new mechanism for a parachute, a collapsible turntable for board games, a quoit ring-toss game.

Sometimes he worked at a desk in the bedroom he shared with his wife. But mostly I heard him in his basement workshop, with its benches, saws, hammers, vises, drill. He occupied himself making furniture while he waited to hear from a patent attorney, from a manufacturer. Out of Masonite he made a file cabinet with the medical caduceus emblazoned on it, a small desk, a chest of drawers, matching bookcases. Out of white pine he made two toy chests, stilts, and a child-size table and chairs for the bedroom Mike and I shared. On one wall of the basement workshop he tacked copies of the letters he wrote and the letters of rejection he received. I would hear him down there punching the basketball-size speed bag that hung from the ceiling. *Yada-yada, yada-yada, yada-yada, yada-yada* . . .

He withdrew from almost every social situation in his wife's work world, and our home was closed to outsiders—there was virtually no entertaining. His long unemployment was humiliating because his wife, Dr. Dunn, supported the family. While aware of her gift of time, he had the feeling again of being trapped—by his sudden family, by the month-by-month expectation of progress on the work front, which he saw in his wife's eyes even if it wasn't there. All my years growing up I never saw them hold hands, put arms around each other.

Day after day while our father worked in the basement, my brother and I played or napped upstairs. Bessie lived with us for about a year and then we

From a draft of Gil's 1951 federal tax return, where he had to write that he was unemployed. His social security number has been blacked out.

Summer 1952.

had daytime caregivers. When a day woman was fired or left, our father had to fill in taking care of us. All his minding of us is lost to memory except one vignette. He had bathed us together in the tub; maybe I was four and Mike three. There was no play in the tub, just soaping, rinsing. Then he plucked us up, stood us on the mat, and waved the white towel lengthwise at us. He did not whip it exactly, but he did wave it briskly, brusquely; the breeze it created was cold. He did not crouch to our level and towel us down, hugging. We were hairless animals, we were a job.

A car trip to visit grandparents was the typical summer family vacation in my early years. Before starting out midmorning, my parents would sit in the living room and have a highball—ginger ale and William Penn rye whiskey. During the hundreds of miles of travel Mike and I always made too much noise, and our father ordered us to be silent. In the dark approaching Gram's he would say to Glad: "We need to stop and get milk and bread; your mother never has anything in the house." Which was not true. I have found only one photo of us as a family of four. Gram took it on the back steps of her house in Ogdensburg when I was six and Mike five.

In 1952 one of our mother's colleagues, a physician who was a war refugee from Latvia, told her about a woman who had kept house for him and his wife in the old country and had followed them in their 1944 escape to

Anna, forty-seven, in 1961.

Germany, to United Nations displaced person camps after the war, and finally to Concord. So Anna Obsenieks came to our house. Mike and I were sitting at the small table in our room. I was wearing corduroy overalls, so was Mike. Anna looked at us and nodded her head. Our father explained that she knew very little English.

Anna lived with us for almost twenty years. She learned an English all her own, "TB" for "TV" and "fidiculous" for "ridiculous." Not that she was a great talker. Her room was in the basement, asbestos-wrapped pipes overhead and cement floor, and you reached it by walking under the indoor clothesline, past two dusty golf bags and a wall stacked with empty ginger ale bottles. She was our housekeeper, making all meals, baking, doing laundry and ironing, bed making, house cleaning. And she watched over my brother and me. But she did not play with us, read to us, or drive us anywhere (she never learned to drive). Anna was a steady, emotionally neutral person; she was not motherly, she did not hug or kiss us. Our father was always "Mr. Dunn" and our mother was "Doctor."

Refugees in the Garden

Winters I nestled in snow caves
and Anna kept an eye on me
out the kitchen window. I dug my cave
near the doctors' garage, steam-heated,
twelve stalls long. Drain pipes plumed,
their drip pocked the snow, and I breathed
hot rusty smells, the scent familiar: the way
air could turn dangerous inside our house.
Come spring, the pipes dried up
and I saw black mouths, guns on watch
along the shingled wall. And it was back here
in the building's long shadow, hidden from view
that Anna made her garden
on the narrow strip between garage
and the fence that bordered us from town.

The garden faced northeast toward Latvia.
Every afternoon she worked land
that wasn't hers, in a country
that could never be home.
Each year she claimed another stall's worth,
pitched her fork to pry out
heavy New Hampshire stones.
She was the first woman I saw sweat,
it gleamed off her round arm muscles
down her thick neck.

I had my own plot, three by four.
She showed me how to set heel
against spade, thrust and turn
rock out of the earth.
We worked in silence.
We never talked about the war

that brought her to this place
and we never talked about my father:
we gardened against our histories.

Come August Anna aproned
emerged from the kitchen
to set out in front of us
platters of fat tomatoes, red as blood,
and tiny ears of sweet stunted corn.

By the year of Anna's arrival, Gil Dunn had conceived an invention with
potential . . . a tray for feeding wild birds at the window. He applied for a patent for this platform feeder, which he named the Flight Deck, after the deck
on aircraft carriers from which pilots took off. Now, knowing more about my
father's difficulty "getting to work," I realize how much Glad must have encouraged him. Certainly her financing was substantial encouragement, because
her earnings paid for his patent applications, attorney fees, and later all costs
of setting up a business—renting space, purchasing equipment as well as raw
materials and parts to build inventory. I never thought to ask her about this,
and of course my father would never have discussed such a topic.

His Work

In 1948 his khaki uniforms hang in the attic,
he works each day at a bench in the basement.
He designs games and gadgets no company wants.
Months, then years, pass: five tax returns
with his wife's earnings list him *unemployed.*
In the postwar boom, no boom for him,
he works wood, smokes, goes fishing.

He sees goldfinches fly across the yard,
flocks of evening grosbeaks
settling high in the trees.
He tinkers with a tray for wild birds

to feed up close—at the window.
Out of the crash on Wall Street,
the Depression, the War,
family life closing in on him,
he squeezes out this one idea
to throw himself into:
    to patent his design,
    to jigsaw and paint Masonite green,
    assemble hardware and dowel packets,
    place small ads in *House Beautiful*,
    Better Homes and Gardens, the *New York Times*.
He works alone in an old brick mill
by a river in a rundown town, and
his one-man mail-order business
and the rest of his life are born.

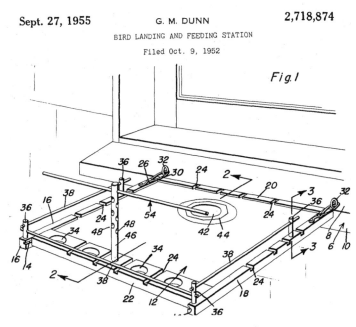

Gil's first patent was issued in 1955—there were at least four more
over the years.

The first shop in Penacook, New Hampshire.

Gil started his own manufacture in rented quarters alongside the Contoocook River in Penacook, a small village seven miles north of Concord. All spring and summer he built inventory, making the bird feeders by hand, spray painting them green in his small paint room, assembling hardware, boxing the product, and stacking the boxes. In the fall and early winter, as orders arrived in response to his small magazine and newspaper advertisements, he labeled and affixed postage stamps on each package himself.

Penacook's Newest Industry Is Really One for the Birds, read the headline on the *Penacook Advertiser*'s front page in January 1953. The article mentioned that Gil Dunn was demonstrating his bird feeder design at Boston's Jordan Marsh department store as part of "New Hampshire Week." As the years went on, he designed more bird feeders and houses and began to sell birdseed and bird-themed gift items from a black-and-white catalog, which he mailed once a year. The business was geared to cold-weather bird feeding and holiday gift-giving, making every autumn an intense time when all the marketing dollars were spent and all the orders needed to be shipped.

After a few years Gil decided to produce all his designs in durable plastic—which required substantial investment in metal molds, and manufacture in Massachusetts. The funds for the capital equipment came solely from Glad's earnings, as the fledgling business was running in the red. Money was tight, so Mike and I didn't get tricycles until a neighbor's kids outgrew theirs and our father could buy them secondhand. We were too big for them within months. I told Mother I no longer wanted dance lessons, and my reason, which I did not tell her, was the cost, a dollar a month back then. I intuited there was no money to spare.

Looking back I see how important the year 1952 was for our family: my father launched his business, and Anna joined our household. I can remember my father telling me the name he created for the company—Duncraft, embedding most of our last name, and echoing brand names such as Chris-Craft boats and the Childcraft set of books, from which Mother read to us stories about the Pied Piper of Hamlin and King Arthur. How gratifying for him at long last to create a company name, find space to rent, outfit a workshop, build inventory, devise an advertising campaign, fill orders. He must have been happy to leave the house, drive to Penacook, and unlock his premises overlooking the river. At forty-two he was his own boss at last. No one was going to oversee him, no one was going to let him go.

Both Mike and I looked like our father. We three had the same Irish coloring, early blond then reddish hair, freckles, rosy cheeks, skin that sunburned. There is no question that my father favored me. Beginning when I was in grade school, during some vacations he took me, never Mike, to work with him.

Penacook was then a sleepy village. Its main industry was an old tannery across the street from Gil's shop. Heaps of cured leather sat in the tannery

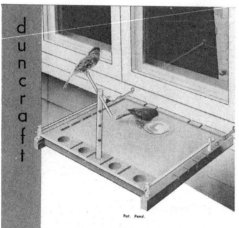

*Magazine advertisement (left top), a
brochure, and an early Duncraft catalog.*

yards, and the air always smelled acrid. We climbed broad dusty stairs to the second floor of a warehouse, to its central space with workbenches for assembly and shipping. A smaller room had a desk, a map of the United States with blue- and red-ended map tacks to show where last season's orders came from, a bulletin board with letters from customers. He set up a workstation at a thick wooden bench: I sat atop a red leather barstool seat, and for hours I assembled packets of hardware. I was proud to be taken to work by my daddy, though I did not like the work itself. At eight years old I was bored and weary after hours of repetitious work. But: I had been chosen.

Mail Order

You work alone at the shop
on the second floor over the grocery.
It smells of sawdust, paint and rain.
On school vacations I come with you
and at the shipping table you show me
what I will do.
    Your hands
dwarf mine, wrapping screws in cellophane.
You fill the window feeders
and the evening grosbeaks flock
as soon as your back is turned.
    Hours go by.
This is a small town, no traffic, no noise.
Only the flutter of black and yellow wings.
At lunchtime you turn on the radio.
I smooth the waxed paper
and finger a jewel of grape jelly
from the edges of the bread.
    We work till five,
you in the back room spraying feeders,
me separating labels saying
Fragile, This End Up, Do Not Crush.

Often I felt a wordless sympathy with my father, as if he and I were alike, not my mother and I. This was fantasy. I identified with an orderliness I perceived in him, a clean style, and a deft economical humor—I made much of little.

Recently my closest friend told me that the day before her wedding her father took her shopping for her wedding shoes. It's inconceivable that my father would engage in such a thoughtful, tender chore with me and for me. When I was thirteen he paid for me to take a two-week typing course at the Concord Commercial College downtown. When I "graduated" as the youngest in the class, he had me spend the rest of the summer in his workshop typing his entire mailing list, fifty thousand names. The next year I was happy that my Candy Striper volunteer work at the general hospital's coffee shop morphed into a summer job as a short-order cook.

One July in my teen years I'd just cleared the dinner dishes, and Anna carried in the birthday cake she had baked for me from scratch, luscious yellow cake with dark chocolate frosting, my favorite. I had a slice. So scrumptious! When I asked for another slice, my father stated the options: not having another piece, or, eating the rest of the two-layer cake—three-quarters remained. He meant, but didn't say, that I was too fat to have a second slice, but if I chose to be gluttonous, then I had to eat "the whole damn thing." This echoed his frequent reluctance, with raised eyebrows, to give my mother a second helping at dinner, because she was overweight. I shoved mean moments like this one aside, or I tried, because I wanted to highlight instead wondrous glimmers that happened only every now and then: him joshing my girlfriends, my working with him in Penacook, or the one or two times he took me fishing.

Daddy's Girl

On the porch
in evening heat
we lay in wait,
a father and his girl,
for the break
of summer storms:
sheets of rain
whipping the beeches,
turning leaves

on their backsides,
for their water-beating.

In the dark
we lay on recliners,
radio tuned to
the Red Sox game.
He loved storms.
I half loved them.
Thunder boomed
through me,
lightning flashed
on his calm face.

I was the quiet
companion
on the porch,
the one he took to work
on school vacations,
the one he took fishing
for river bass in a secret spot,
a few Sunday afternoons,
the daughter,
not the son.

    In his youth Gil Dunn had been passionate about canoeing. What happened to that passion? In our grandparents' backyard in Mahopac I saw a canoe stored upside down on trestles; we could have trailered that canoe home. But we did no boating of any kind though we lived in a state renowned for its many lakes. Perhaps it was a matter of money again, everything extra going to the business. In my later high school years my father purchased a small aluminum rowboat, which he could fit in the back of his station wagon; this allowed him to fish on a pond rather than from the banks of the Merrimack River. He never talked about the canoeing and racing of his youth—another part of himself hidden away. A love of his, forsaken—and never shared with his children.

Mother

In 1948 and for several years, Gladys Dunn was the only female psychiatrist on staff at the New Hampshire State Hospital. She conducted mental health clinics in eleven small cities all over the state, and treated patients on her days on the hospital campus, attended staff meetings, taught nurses, supervised social workers, testified in court. When she came home in the evenings, all of us, children and our father, wanted her attention. After her workday Glad never had enough time for us or for herself.

My sense now is that most of the time my mother was overwhelmed. Maybe after scores of patients, personnel issues, hospital politics, she just couldn't deal with the toxicity of our every dinnertime. It was hard for her to get up many mornings. Her clothes were piled in a midden on the chair in the bedroom and were jammed into her closet. Her bureau top was a clutter of nail polishes, emery boards, perfume bottles, overflowing ashtrays, costume jewelry, stray coins, tobacco dust. Her side table in the living room likewise was laden with books, newspapers folded to the crossword puzzle, more nail polishes, letters, bills, stationery. In contrast, my father's bureau drawers were neat as if he had a valet, his few clothes hung straight in the closet, his side table in the living room had only the latest *Business Week* and an ashtray. He could have packed one large suitcase and it would have contained all his possessions in our house.

While our mother had no time to be involved in our school lives and never knew our teachers, at home she was nurturing and warm. When we were little she read to us at bedtime; and she pretended that we were loaves of bread that had to bake overnight in our beds: she would knead our blanketed bodies and plump us into shape, and I remember she would touch me lightly with her fingernail and say, "Ah, an air bubble!" She would crayon a whole page in my coloring book when I was asleep, leaving it for me as a surprise. On Saturdays she walked downtown with us; we ate egg salad sandwiches at the Liggett Drug Store, shopped at Newberry's, and saw an afternoon movie. She included me in décor decisions—shall we have the living room papered in two different patterns? We cooked together on Anna's weekends off.

Children

Mike and I spent a great amount of time out of the house. This was our antidote to its toxicity. Paradoxically, we felt safe biking or walking all over the mental hospital grounds or running in the underground tunnels that connected the huge brick buildings, but we felt unsafe inside our house. We burrowed into snow caves, sledded on the hill behind Tobey Building with its wards of chronically ill men, skated for hours at a small ice rink behind the nurses' dormitory or later on the large public pond in town. Summers we climbed the elephantine limbs of the beech trees in our backyard, we swam at a municipal pool. We created a network of hideouts all over the hospital grounds with the Burbank kids, whose father was the grounds superintendent, and the Penhale boys, whose dad was a family doctor in town. Our Green Leaf hideout nestled near the hundred wooden stairs scaling the hill to Brown Building with its wards of aged women patients. Another, Stone Bridge, lay by the greenhouses and tennis courts. We were graced with our life outside the house—fresh air, exercise, friends—and by the not infrequent contact with other parents, who were so different from our own. Mrs. Burbank drove us to go swimming at Keyser Lake on summer weekends and invited me for dinner any night, and Dr. Penhale showed an interest in Mike, enjoying his elfin humor.

In his teens Mike found the Assembly of God church, where he became part of a new community. I volunteered at the general hospital, joined the Girl Scouts, babysat, attended Sunday school and taught second graders at the Congregational church, and took long walks in the countryside with my friend Susan. I spent hours playing tennis, many hours at the public library, and stayed after school editing the high school newspaper. Both Mike and I created different selves, with self-esteem, outside the home.

Recently Mike and I were talking on the phone about our childhood. He said, "Remember the time he took all your pencils and lined them up end to end on the floor, out of your room, down the hall, down the stairs, across the downstairs hall, into the living room?" No, I didn't remember. Mike said, "It was his way of saying that you had too many pens and pencils." Mike also told me about reading sessions on the screened porch when he was about seven, which I never knew took place. Mike struggled (he was dyslexic) with the *Weekly Reader*, unable to read the word *iron*. Our father made him try to sound out the word "fifty, a hundred times," Mike said, "and I couldn't go play until I could read it. He just wouldn't let me go." Mike also got belt whipped a good deal—it was terrible to hear his cries from his bedroom. For he was not a bad child, just an energetic boy making his own way through childhood with little attention from his humorless working parents and a housekeeper who barely spoke English.

What does a father feel when he is rethreading his belt in his trouser loops? When he turns his back and closes the door on a child sobbing on a bed or cowering in a corner? What did my father feel? Inner release? Grim satisfaction that the "misbehavior" or "infraction" of the son was "corrected"?

I was no ally for my brother: if I had stood up for Mike I might have come in for the same treatment from our father, so I stayed out of it. But I was witness. I stewed in feelings: relief it wasn't me, guilt that it wasn't me, empathy for my brother's struggles, hatred of my father for his tyranny, for the injustice, and a profound bafflement about why my mother did nothing.

In my conversations by phone with Mike, sharing memories, I have learned important pieces of our story. My brother revealed how he got through the many harangues our father delivered: Mike would look at a spot just a little beyond the angry head and stare at it. This is how he dealt with the vituperation—it flowed past him, not through him. And he told me that by the time he was a teen, he said to himself, "This is a crazy man. I'm staying out of his way." I see now that my brother arrived at a strategy that worked for him and a judgment I never came close to.

Where was my father's empathy? Once when I had to sleep on the porch in summer (his parents were visiting and occupied my room), I felt lonely. Though crying myself to sleep every night was usual for me, this night in the semi-outdoors my crying was almost hysterical and it was audible. The door opened. Would someone comfort me? "What do you have to cry about? Stop this sniveling at once," my father said, and went back inside.

When I was fifteen Mother brought home a dachshund puppy. We settled him in a cardboard box in the kitchen for his first night, with a ticking clock for company and an old bed jacket of my mother's as a cozy. The light was flicked off, the kitchen doors shut. After a while the little dog started whining. We were watching TV and I offered to check on him. "Stay where you are," my father ordered. "He's whining for attention, that's all." My father forbade us to go to him, "to teach him a lesson." Finally when my father went to bed, Mother and I found Dizzy with his nose stuffed way up inside the sleeve of the bed jacket and exhausted from trying to extricate himself.

My father was extraordinarily sensitive to slights. Mother drove me home from minor surgery when I was thirteen. Getting out of the car, with a patch on my eye, I reached out to calm Dizzy, who barked joyously and scrambled to greet me. My father was miffed that he took second place to our dog, and he let me know it by turning and walking into the house without a word.

What Was Hidden

November and December—the "busy season" for my father's business—were very hard months. Gil would get up at 4:00 a.m. and be at the shop by 5:00. He would come home at 6:30 p.m. and go to bed by 9:00. His eyes grew bloodshot, his temper short, and he often caught a terrible cold that turned into bronchitis, surely aggravated by his heavy smoking. He soldiered on, wearing himself out, only to find out when the season closed that again he had not made a profit. This happened year after year.

This sad fact, his lack of financial success and plenty, contrasted not only with his parents' situation of ease but also his sister Muriel's comfortable life. Muriel married Bill Tooley, the Army captain, and they settled in Hawthorne, New York, not far from her parents in Mahopac. Like her mother, Muriel was a "stay-at-home mom." Bill Tooley worked for the famed Robert Moses on infrastructure projects in New York City. When I was a child I had no inkling of what Uncle Bill did, but certainly my father knew that his brother-in-law was manager for the construction of Shea Stadium and later was its first director. Bill helped arrange the helicopter arrival of the Beatles at the World's Fair site in Queens, and their ride in a Wells Fargo van to the stadium in August 1965 for the first rock concert ever held in such a venue. My cousin recently wrote me that she was in her father's office the afternoon Jackie Kennedy stopped by and left her umbrella. We never heard these stories! Many years later, as a young adult, I visited Uncle Bill at his last job—president of the East Side Terminal in New York City—and was surprised that he was an executive in a corner office with a view. No one mentioned that Bill and Muriel flew to Florida on holiday in winter, and vacationed in Amagansett on Long Island in summer. As a child on visits to them, I experienced their two daughters, one my age, another four years younger, as the center of the household—they could drink Pepsi, they went to private school, their parents drove them here and there as a matter of course. The four Tooleys went bowling together every Saturday. Aunt Muriel and Uncle Bill adored their children, really enjoyed them.

Gil knew he was not the success his father and his brother-in-law were. However, no one but he and my mother knew that at the end of every "busy season" the business barely broke even, if that. To Mike and me, to anyone else in the family, and to the world, Gil Dunn shipped his patented products all over the country, and he owned and ran his own business. In some sense, the business was his cover—he could appear to be successful, to be his own man.

How did my father feel working for years in Penacook, driving the seven miles along old Route 3? Yes, he was content working alone, in control of all aspects of his work. The shop was really his haven, his world; he knew people in the village—from Toots, who operated the gas station next door, to Bob, who owned the insurance agency. The shop expressed him, everything from how the counters out front displayed product for the few customers who stopped in, to the Mallomars in the side drawer of his army green metal desk. Interestingly, in the shop, unlike at home, his desk was a mess. The tiny bathroom had only cold water. I think that at moments—and he had many, in his solitude—he fell into hopelessness; his achievement did not match his expectations, his efforts were wheels spinning with no traction. In his impoverishment, in his anger, he continually took the shards of his disappointment and projected them onto others. Then he saw shortcomings, faults and flaws, in the other. The first "other" I know of was my mother—back when Gil made life intolerable for her when she was first pregnant and she responded by leaving him. Next, and for much longer, the prime "other" was my brother.

Our father treated us as objects—maybe not all the time, but most of the time. I've recently been rereading Henry James's *The Portrait of a Lady*. Isabel Archer finally realizes in horror that her husband *uses* her; she is tool or thing, not a person for him. I can reflect now on how Mike and I "served" our father. Mike's whole being became a screen onto which Gil could project the film of his failures, and Gil could then scorn Mike, lord over him, and establish himself as superior and powerful. Me? I was the thornless Sharon Rose. For my father I was a pondlike mirror. I emanated propitiation, admiration, serenity, and compliance, to supply him what he thirsted for. This became second nature to me.

When Anna had her one weekend off a month, my mother and I would sit at the kitchen table for breakfast on Saturday mornings. My father had already driven to Penacook, my brother was still asleep upstairs. Maybe I was ten when I started to ask my mother why we had "to live like this." *Why was my father so cruel to Mike? Why was every dinnertime harrowing? Why did we have to stay together?* She never gave me an answer. She would say: *You must understand.* Now I realize what she would not say to me: that she knew my father was a damaged man, he had no way to support himself without her, and he had little resilience of character. Early she had ceded him the role of head of the house, empowering him who had no power outside the home; she did not foresee how his unconscious needs—to project his self-hatred, to be soothed by compliance—would abuse that power and shadow her children's lives.

I think that, as a psychiatrist, she knew Gil had a personality structure that offered little or no hope of change. He was a person to be worked around, managed around, not changed. She was patient, she lowered her own expectations of reciprocity, she probably protected Mike and me in ways we never saw. She counseled that I *understand*—this was her way of saying I had to accept our family life. It would not change.

9: Endings

What did I love about my father? For despite his flaws and failings, I did love him deeply. He was manly—with a lean meatiness, strong hands, muscled shoulders and back. He was always groomed and smelled faintly of Astring-O-Sol and Brylcreem. I loved how neat he was—this is what I saw at home—how good he looked in khakis and a Pendleton wool shirt or in a white starched shirt with cuff links. He wore a heavy silver chain bracelet with a plate engraved with his Army serial number, which of course I memorized: 12021733. He drove the car authoritatively, with relaxed hands low on the steering wheel. Yes, I see I recount physical details because my sensory experience of him is the strongest positive memory I have of him. But also, I did feel for the man who came home every night with the worn briefcase, who kept at the business year after year, who set up a card table outdoors on Sunday afternoons in summer to work on costs and pricing, who hung new feeder designs in the beech trees in the backyard. I truly felt that I, better than anyone in the world, understood him.

When my parents discussed my going to college, my father said: Why does Sharon need to go to college? And there, right there, is the chasm between me and him, my world and his. He was proud that I got top grades, but he was unaware that I was in a college preparatory program in my public high school, that I waseditor-in-chief of the school newspaper, on the debate team, and so on. I was the "apple of his eye"—yet that was because I succeeded in being a compliant daughter in the realm of the house—and that was his goal for me, that was my highest achievement. He liked me because I tried to please him. He had no idea of what was going on in my life, my interests, my dreams. His world had a seven-mile diameter: he was focused inward on himself, his business, and he did not really pay much attention to anything else. All that intelligence of his burrowed inward. For my mother there was absolutely no

*Gil, at Christmas-
time, about 1967,
with a rare guest in
our home.*

question that I was going to college. That issue was settled, though there were grumbles from my father about tuition payments.

I said that I never had a real conversation with my father. Well, there was one, but it was more a baring of the heart than a conversation. It was my freshman year at college, the spring. My mother unexpectedly came to visit me for an hour on a Sunday at my dormitory in Medford, Massachusetts. She had never visited before. We sat in the large parlor and talked; she'd been on a short get-away road trip with a woman she worked with. Unusual for her. She looked tired, her skin sallow. My spring break would begin that Friday, I'd be home, I'd see her again soon, I said. Something surprising happened: that Tuesday my father phoned (he had never phoned before) to tell me he would come to drive me home at the end of the week, rather than my taking the bus from downtown Boston as I always had before. On the seventy-mile drive to Concord he told me that my mother had suffered a massive heart attack the night after her visit to me. She was going to be all right, he said.

After seeing her pale and weak inside an oxygen tent in the hospital room, I went home and drew a bath, and lying there, my body grew limp, all energy sapped. It would take months for her to recover, the rest of spring, the whole summer. I was sad, angry, and afraid. We were fortunate that she would live, but she was lost to me as a confidante. I could not burden her with my troubles, the boyfriend relentlessly pursuing me, my quandary over what profession I should prepare for. Medicine? Language studies? I needed her wisdom but could not ask for it. Now I think: Was my father in fear of what would happen to his life? What if Glad never worked again, was not able to support him and the business? Did he care about her, her suffering and her fear?

Yes, Anna cooked dinner, it was on the table at six as always. My brother, a junior in high school, was nowhere to be seen—probably at a friend's house, dealing with all this the best he could. So it was just my father and me at the table.

I said, "In a way it was inevitable, wasn't it?"

"Inevitable?" he repeated.

"Her stress at work—the travel, the workload, the politics of the hospital. And then every day she comes home not to restore herself but to endure your never-ending criticism of Mike. Your oppression of him. You never let up. Never. It's terrible. A terrible way to live." His eyes filled and he wiped his tears with the back of a hand. His shoulders were shaking and he could not speak. I thought, he really must care for her and feel responsible and guilty. This is my one memory of speaking truth to him, and him hearing. But it dropped like a stone into a deep pond. Mother resumed work that autumn. And I never spoke this way to him again.

Yet I have evidence that my mind tends to grip grimness and let go facts that make the story more complex and perplexing. I retrieved from a closet a shoebox of letters from my college years. Mother wrote me that she had gone to a conference in Montreal in the fall after that heart attack: *When I came home I felt so fortunate,* she wrote. *Rene is two years younger than me but I was surprised at the lines in her disappointed face. To have you two children and Daddy is a great happiness, and I do appreciate what good care you all take of me. In comparison to Rene I have few lines in my face and those that are there I think are pleasant ones.* That December my father wrote me: *My dear Little Pumpkin, Great you will be home this Saturday. . . . Not knowing when you will blow into town on the bus, think it best that you jump a taxi (on me of course). This is the most practical arrangement at this time of year, snow, sleet, rumbles, having dinner, drinking grog or taking a bath (which isn't likely). However if there are no taxis in the stall, then phone*

1969, offspring out of the house.

promptly. See you, Love, me. The next month he wrote me a postcard: *Hello Sugar Plum. . . . Won't be long before your little footsteps will be padding to and fro from you know where. Love you, Dad.* The tone is much like his wartime letters to Glad, humorous and deft. And doting. He could express such sweetness only at a distance when he imagined his reader, not a real person but his fantasy of her.

The next years saw my brother and me leaving home for good. Mike began separating earlier than I—in his senior year in high school he worked full-time as a white-uniformed attendant on the 3:00–11:00 p.m. shift on the locked men's ward in the Thayer Building right across the road from our home. As my mother wrote me, *Why not? He doesn't do homework anyway, and he enjoys working!* Within a couple of years Mike and I both married. At home alone with Glad, Gil no longer had competition for her attention. Life was simpler, even better, without Mike and me, and they grew closer. Just before I left to live abroad, I took photos of them sitting together. Gil leaned on the back of Glad's upholstered chair, looking down at her, and she looked up at him with a smile. They had been married almost twenty-five years. Glad and Gil had begun to think about moving off the hospital grounds—they had spotted a house for sale on Apple Tree Lane on the outskirts of the beautiful village of Hopkinton.

But my father's cancer put an end to the dream of owning their own home, and to the peace they had arrived at after so many years. A heavy smoker since sixteen, who bought cigarettes by the carton and never tried to quit smoking, Gil developed a cough that would not go away. X-rays taken in winter 1971 indicated surgery to evaluate his condition. This befell him just at the tail end of a years-long losing battle with the Internal Revenue Service, about which I had been told nothing. The IRS was after Gil because certain expenses had been improperly taken off the business's income. The IRS claimed *intent*, Gil's attorney claimed lack of knowledge of standard bookkeeping practices, *no intent*. The attorney later revealed to me that the IRS agent hounded my father "like Javert pursued Jean Valjean in Hugo's *Les Misérables*." There was a threat of imprisonment, but instead heavy fines were imposed. Gil was embattled, inside and out.

In May 1971 his chest was opened up and the surgeon just stitched him back up after seeing how extensive the cancer was. Still, Gil had radiation treatments that summer. To spell my mother, I flew home from London where I was living. I made my father chocolate ice cream sodas so that he would gain

June 1971.

weight; I accompanied him to the hospital for radiation treatments. Remarkably, I never heard the word *cancer* spoken by him, or to him. He lived moment to moment, he did no planning, and I think, no reflecting, typical of him I now see. Over the next eleven months I flew home another three times. When he was home from one stay at the hospital, we watched evening TV from the couch, and on came the inevitable cigarette ads, which he sat through like a statue. The end table next to him no longer held an ashtray.

After that summer of recovery from surgery and radiation, Gil had a burst of vigor. He had put on weight, felt pretty good, and on my September trip home we set off by car, Mother, Dad, and I, to visit my father's parents and Muriel and Bill. Remarkably, my father drove the whole way. At one point he missed an exit on the Taconic Parkway and backed up in the breakdown lane, and I thought as I sat in the backseat wordless and highly anxious: "Yes, you can risk your life because you have little time left. What about *my* life?" We got there safely, and it was a good visit, everyone was in good spirits, as if nothing were happening. I took what became a favorite photo of my father there. It was the last time he was strong and handsome.

September 1971.

The next time I flew home it was just before Thanksgiving, and he was bedridden. I slow-cooked a turkey overnight. Thanksgiving morning the household woke to a blizzard, and I walked for two hours over the hospital's acres—whitened ground, air, sky, all indistinguishable from one another in the storm. My father ate tiny portions of everything, from a tray. Mother taught me how to give him Demerol injections. A few days later he was hospitalized with an inflamed knee, and he saw Japanese soldiers charge at him through the walls. I had never heard him say anything about Japanese soldiers. Were the terrors of war, like these storming soldiers, always just under the surface of his waking life?

Mother and I worked with the attorney who had handled his tax case, and we arranged for the business to continue. It was put in an irrevocable trust with all income to Glad, a way to defer estate taxes. The plan was that my brother, now a father himself with two children, would manage the business day to day, and I would pitch in with marketing and bookkeeping on weekends—by then I knew I would be returning to live in the States. When

I presented the trust documents to my father to sign I am not sure he knew what they were, or, if he did know, he no longer cared.

Our father wrote on a strip of paper: *Mike hired Jan 1 1972 $10,000*—the first visible sign of regard for Mike, well, acknowledgement of him, that I knew of. Mike remembers he was able to pick up his father from bed by then and bring him to the tub to be bathed.

Twice that March I made plane reservations to come home. The first time I cancelled because I was sick, the second time Mother phoned to say not to come. However, in mid-April Mother called again. I'm now so ashamed of my moments of resentment flying over the Atlantic: Was this one more false alarm about the end? But it wasn't.

He was in his twin bed just looking at the curtains. On my last visit home he had told me that he spent hours making stories out of the furls in the curtains—there was a mountain chain, there a woman's profile, there a wolf's head. Now he was a skeleton. His face gaunt, those narrow lips dry. He was unable to speak any longer and he no longer ate. The afternoon I arrived my mother telephoned eighty-year-old Rose and put the phone to his ear, and he made a dry sound—that was his good-bye to his mother.

It was a warm April day. Mother, perspiring, bustled around the room; we changed his sheets, gently, because it was clear that his whole body was in pain. Then a question I will never forget. My mother said to him, with jaunty affect but really with anxiety, "I know you don't love me, but you do love Sharon, don't you? She's just come home to be with you."

He pressed his lips together and shook his head no.

What did his answer mean? He didn't love me? Or didn't love either of us? Or, he didn't agree with her premise—that in fact he *did* love her? That he couldn't answer the question, so he just shook his head? That he shook his head no, when he meant to nod yes?

So, to the end, they were out of harmony. How could she pose this question to him? How could she expect him, with a cancer-riddled brain, in God knows what degree of pain (he was on morphine and codeine, alternately every two hours), to answer such a question, front-loaded with the assumption that he didn't love her?

Poor Mum. There she was, worn out from months of nursing, from the siege of illness that had overtaken their lives, knowing the signs of oncoming death because she was a physician, knowing she was about to become a widow. She looked so weary, her hair needed cutting, her nails were unpolished. Her question revealed that she believed he did not love her, that he loved only his daughter. She could live with that, though wasn't there faint hope embedded in her question—that he might love her after all?

And me?—the twenty-five-year-old, who had driven to the shop in Pena-cook to see what I could organize there, how we could continue the business. Me, who always felt I was closer to him than anyone else. To have this denial as his last "word" to me . . . I was angry with my mother for her question, and I was devastated by his "answer."

He died the next evening at ten o'clock. Mike, Mother, and I were down-stairs watching *Elmer Gantry* on TV as his last breathing, stentorian, filled the house and then didn't. Mike went up to check, and came down. "He's gone." In the end, he was alone. He was sixty-two years old.

10: Legacy from My Father

My husband, John, who never knew my father, asked me, How did you feel when he died? And I answered: bereft. For, as little as he actually gave me, it was everything I had from him, it was my 100 percent. My love for him was like an Escher drawing; I could not tell where my love began or ended, it just was. For many years it never occurred to me, all that a different father might have given me—true knowing and empathy, encouragement, intellectual companionship, and moments where he might have carefully listened to me.

What legacy did our father Gilbert Dunn leave Michael and me besides the insidious psychological patterns for coping and perceiving that his behavior imprinted on us, which I've recounted in detail earlier?

He left behind a business he created and built over twenty years. He had persisted with this enterprise, and now I could see that the Great Depression had twice undercut Gil's native ability to persevere at work. In those twenty years his Duncraft had established a name, built a customer list, and developed a line of products. Gil left a small nineteenth-century brick building free of mortgage. Inventory. A typewriter, some tools, office supplies, a file cabinet. However, a listing of assets is not a proper reflection of his legacy. Great value lay embedded in that customer list, the line of products, and the concept of a business dedicated to feeding wild birds. His one-man business contained potential energy, ready to release and be set in motion.

~

Family Business
The dead return with suntans to ask questions.

His footsteps scatter the sparrows
pecking at the cracked corn
my brother's sprinkled like salt
on the snowy front steps.
I don't know why the birds
are feeding so late and in the dark.
He finds his way upstairs to my office—
in his time it was a storeroom.
He perches on the edge of my desk
with one question:
What have you two done to my business?

I hand him financial statements.
They mean nothing.
He wants a sense of place—
workbenches, stock shelves,
cartons, parts. He gets up,
roams the building.
I listen to doors open
and close around me
and down below.

It runs without you, Father.
This is what we built
on what you left,
on the one-man business
you kept small,
those twenty years of six-day weeks,
the busy seasons of bloodshot eyes.

Nothing is the same
except the old red safe
where my brother and I keep our wills.
He leaves without a word,

down the steps—scattering
the hungry sparrows—
into the falling snow.

Mike and I doubled sales each of the first five years we ran Duncraft, and it kept growing, though not at that rate, over decades. We computerized processes, we printed the catalog in color, we developed new lines of products. Our mother lived to see the company begin to grow and create profit. To this day, it's mysterious to me how Mike and I, who were often left on the wayside of our parents' lives of all work and no play, ended up continuing the business, no, devoting ourselves to it. Wasn't the business in some sense the child that was nurtured—by our father's single-minded attention and our mother's paychecks?

The business became the "living connection" to our parents when they were gone. We would fulfill their lives—and our own lives—through the business, recast the story and make our father the founder of a thriving enterprise and acknowledge our mother's crucial role as silent funding partner . . . Well, that's the story I would like to tell myself about Mike and me, but it is not the story Mike sees. Mike took on the business wholeheartedly as an opportunity for himself and his family—he was right to imagine he could do much more, and earn more, in the family business than in the inventory management job he had with a large printer in town.

In the early years I worked weekends, focusing on marketing and on our finances, because I was employed as an editor for the Boston Consulting Group in downtown Boston. I took evening classes in accounting and managerial finance at Boston University School of Management. Mike worked every day at the office in Penacook: he excelled at operations. My skills in marketing and planning complemented his skills; eventually I worked full-time for the family business, working on-site a few days a week and the rest of the time from my home in Cambridge, Massachusetts. My brother and I were two ragged halves of a gypsy's broken medallion, but we fit together perfectly.

25 South Main Street

The little depressed business
we decided to run
surprised us. Sales doubled
each year, year upon year.
We were such different children
but now, we were working partners,
you doing day-to-day,
me marketing.

You lived up the hill
in the mill owner's Victorian,
I drove up from Cambridge
for two days each week.
You could be the boss
and I could live where
I wanted: anywhere
but there.

Oh that early year,
we sat in a restaurant one night
and split in two the company's
unbelievable profit. We were
greedy children
suddenly fed
something so rich
and we ate and ate and ate.

Eventually I stayed with the business because I found it challenging as the
company grew in complexity, and I also had my own family to support. And
Mike grew into his own as an accomplished man of business.

~

Sister and brother portrait for the Duncraft catalog, 1997.

So, after all this digging and mulling, do I have a clearer idea of how my father became the unhappy, acidly critical person I knew? At ten he was the joyful woodchuck hunter, later a passionate canoeist with many pals. He was the Wall Street clerk with prospects, a Hoover manager of forty men, a crew chief selected for a special mission. Passages from his letters and journal reveal a talented wordsmith; but his skill at writing was a buried talent—I never knew we shared a love of language, never imagined this was part of my legacy from him. He was intelligent, handsome, and constitutionally strong (his parents and sister lived into their late eighties). But he lost those jobs in the Great Depression and was out of work for years under his father's dark eye; he survived painful meningitis but suffered long-term side effects from it, and later was injured in an auto accident. After two years seeing front-line action in World War II, he returned a thirty-five-year-old veteran with psychological issues, seemingly no marketable skills, and not even a high school degree. Eventually he became an entrepreneur of a one-man company that never made money, and he was a husband and disengaged father in a house where he only ate, slept, and watched TV.

With her single comment years ago my grandmother revealed her husband Martin's ever-critical eye on Gil. Was Gil shaped or deformed by a demanding father, not seen for who he was, but for who his father wanted him to be, and always falling short? Constant criticism, not being recognized for oneself, carves fissures in a personality and prompts many defenses. Financially dependent during much of the Depression and emotionally close to his mother, Gil did not set off on his own; he stayed in the household where his father held him in contempt. Gil's years at war tipped whatever balance he had: he saw death and injury up close, he lived with fear, ennui, hunger. These stresses deepened the fissures and made his defenses stronger, made him less flexible.

My father lived a tyranny of never-ending compulsions. He *had* to lock up or project out the bitter self-hatred brewed by failure, disappointments, and lack of success. What a lot of energy that took. He constantly *had* to acquire a supply of good feeling about himself—by mainlining outright admiration or by crushing someone else to experience his superiority.

Growing up I never conceived of my father as emotionally ill. I carried inside me a fearsome, powerful father and now, as I've pieced together his story, the person who has emerged is a man whose self was injured and misshapen, who salvaged self-respect in unconscious and damaging ways. I remember his saying to me once that he would rather be respected than loved. That was incomprehensible to me then. But I understand now: it was self-respect he hungered for.

Paradoxically—and I find myself shaking my head—what kept him stabilized was the encompassing surround and support that our mother gave him—at great cost to herself, to Mike, and to me.

Now I mourn for the man he might have been, had *he* had a different father and more good fortune in life. Good fortune such as not inheriting the gene for color blindness, not contracting meningitis, and, especially, living in better economic times. He had so many native gifts and strengths. Maybe Gil could have been a successful commercial artist in Manhattan despite his color blindness, a man who kept good friends from his younger years and made new ones, who canoed and eventually took up sailing on his own boat moored on City Island. Maybe he wouldn't marry, maybe he would enjoy being a loving uncle to Muriel's girls, arriving in Hawthorne with gifts every holiday and birthday. Or maybe he would marry a lighthearted woman more like his sister. He would feel both joy and pleasure because he was content with his accomplishments, and he was grounded by self-respect. And I mourn for the actual man, the man I knew, who suffered within his contorted inner world.

For so long I have been stuck in the remembrance of childhood with my guilt, my anger, my questions. I always felt guilty that Mike had to endure so much at the hand of our father, far more, I thought, than I. Being at Mike's side in the business was my reparation, served over a long time and finally paid. By unearthing my father's past and piecing together his story, by imagining his emotional landscape, much of my anger has dissipated, replaced mostly by sorrow for his sad life. The childhood I look back on now has more light shining onto it, into it, through it, because I have answers to the central question of how my father became the man he was.

Recently I had a dream in which I was inside my childhood home, that modest brick duplex, on the hospital grounds in New Hampshire, and a contemporary friend in my life now, a documentary filmmaker named Adam, looked wide-eyed at the rooms, and said to me, "Wow, your Dad sure did a good job . . ."

I said firmly: "My father did not build this house," and I went on to tell my friend that the house was constructed as a WPA project in the Roosevelt era.

This dream is telling me that my father did not make my life, I have made my life, I have made the self I live in. It has been my work in progress. Despite the damage our father inflicted, both my brother and I have gone on to lead good lives. For myself, I found running the business intellectually challenging and satisfying; I liked working on strategy, analyzing numbers, leading teams, hiring bright people, creating a brand, and heading marketing. Perhaps running the business did serve to keep me psychologically close to my father and brother; I see that making the business successful also allowed me to surpass and vanquish my father, a very unconscious project. And because it never occurred to me before his illness that I would have anything to do with the business, never did I have an intimation that Mike and I would together create financial plenty, assuring our own and our families' comfort and security. Ultimately, I sold my share of the company to my brother; now Michael owns Duncraft entirely, directing it and working on projects he enjoys.

I managed to fulfill my love of language and literature by editing and publishing a nonprofit literary magazine of fiction and poetry, and by writing poems myself. The adolescent girl I was hardly dared dream that I would live and travel abroad, undergo psychoanalysis, build a successful business, write books, own my own home, marry for love, become a mother. Yet I did all these.

At the end of my search for my father I feel I have earned what I felt forever: that I know my father better than anyone else. My fantasy had been that in writing his story I would awaken his spirit and that his spirit would be transformed, knowing he had been seen at last. But that is a wish. The reality is that he was the way he was. The transformation is in my seeing.

My Mother, Once a Remarkable Life

Part Two

11: Where Glad Came From

No sooner did I come to the end of writing about my father than I knew I was not finished with this family story. What about my mother? Could I unravel the part my mother the psychiatrist played in our family drama? How did she come to, or fall into, her complicated role? How did her family shape her, what were her values, her life experiences? Earlier I briefly described my mother and her work, but I did not look at her formative years as I dived into my father's life. Now I want to know more about her life and times and why she married Gil Dunn, then stayed in that marriage, and—I know this seems hyperbolic, but I can't think of another way of putting it—why she did not "save" my brother and me.

In the few years after her retirement, Mother and I talked every week, over dinners and breakfasts when I worked in New Hampshire at the family business and stayed overnight with her. Why didn't I pose my questions to her then? Well, I have an answer to that. We were occupied not with the past but with the present. Her postretirement years were riddled with serious health issues: several heart attacks, a minor stroke, diabetes, glaucoma. Also, she was caught up in my brother's family life: four, then five small grandchildren living in the main house and dropping in to see Grammy. As for me, I was tangled in my love life and I was ambitious for the business as well as the literary magazine I ran and for my first poems. There was so much in the present to talk about. Or is that rationalization? Were we afraid of what we might discover? The fact is: we left the elephant under the carpet. Now, decades later I find myself trying to make sense of her life and the choices she made.

Her name, Gladys, is Welsh. Who knows where her parents, neither of whom had any Welsh heritage, got it. She was always called Glad, or Glady, which she sometimes spelled as Gladdy, and I called her Mum. Outside our house she was Dr. Dunn. I knew some of my mother's story from her and from her younger sister, but I also have learned from letters, photographs, and newspapers. From a humble uneducated family, Gladys Ward became their hero by entering medical school in 1929 and embarking on a promising career as a psychiatrist in the mid-1930s. It was her marriage to Gilbert Dunn that turned a visibly remarkable life into an invisibly tragic one.

Glad's parents, when young, and their parents before them, and theirs before them, lived in poverty—not different from my father's Irish and Scandinavian forebears. The setting is Ogdensburg in St. Lawrence County in northern New York State. This city of approximately twelve thousand inhabitants is located on the south bank of the Saint Lawrence River, across which you can see Canada. Gladys Ward was born there in 1907, child of two immigrant populations that crossed the river from Canada to the United States: French Canadians and the Irish-English-Scots.

I'll go into some detail about the families Glad came from because I think that their hard history shaped her. Her father Edward's mother, Josephine Denny, was born in Quebec and spoke only French. The immigrant Denny family of eleven lived in the very poorest part of Ogdensburg and was left destitute when Josephine's father froze to death trying to find work across the river in Canada. At sixteen Josephine Denny gave birth out of wedlock. A few years later she married a man named Fred Ward. Near the end of his life, my grandfather, Edward Ward, applying for a passport, saw his birth certificate for the first time. He was shocked: there was Josephine Denny as *mother*, but the space for *father* was blank. My grandfather did not know he had been adopted by Fred Ward, a laborer of French Canadian heritage, who was a drinker. His mother never revealed to him his biological father.

I've traced Josephine Denny's ancestors back to the mid-1600s, to six *filles du roi*—daughters of the king—given dowries and sent by King Louis XIV to help populate New France: they were poor but chaste young women from Normandy and Paris, willing to the leave the Old World that held no future for them and sail to the New World and marry farmers, soldiers, and trappers. It's highly probable that other *filles du roi* contributed to the genetic makeup of Edward's biological father; I have deduced he was French Canadian by having my own DNA analyzed.

As seventeen-year-olds, my mother's parents, Edward Ward and Mildred Hanratty, fell in love and married in Ogdensburg's Roman Catholic Notre

*Minnie Hanratty at
sixteen.*

Dame church in 1904. In the online church records I found their names represented as "Eduoard LaGuerre" and "Melina Henrietta" for the Mass in French and Latin. As I explained earlier, the French surname LaGuerre, meaning "war," was Americanized into the English name Ward. The couple settled in the town of Oswagatchie, a poor section of Ogdensburg near the Oswagatchie River, which flowed into the Saint Lawrence. Edward worked first as a bottler in a brewery, then as bookkeeper for a liquor dealer; he himself, my mother told me, never drank.

As a girl and young woman, Glad's mother, Mildred, was called Minnie. She was one of eight Hanrattys raised in the countryside of the nearby village of Lisbon, New York. Minnie's paternal grandfather emigrated from tenant farmland in County Monaghan, north of Dublin, and Minnie's mother's people were poor farm folk from English Canada. At the age of eight Minnie was sent away to a farming couple in a nearby village to work for room and board because her own family could not feed her; among her chores were to bring in wood for the stove, start the fire in early morning, and prepare the bread dough. She cried herself to sleep at night because she was lonely and the work was beyond her strength. Next she served in the home of a spinster school-teacher, and woke up Christmas morning to see a "miraculous" orange set out for her on the bedside table. By the time she was a teen, Minnie and a sister were live-in servants for a wealthy couple in Ogdensburg, for fifty cents a week each. Around this time Minnie Hanratty met Edward Ward at the Canton Fair, where her father, Abe, had a stable on the fairgrounds and raced horses.

My grandmother was pushed out of her family and set to work at an early age. I wondered what *her* mother's experience was. Well, Minnie's mother, Hattie, was only five years old when *her* mother died giving birth to her ninth child. At sixteen, Hattie, new immigrant from Canada, was a live-in servant for a family in Lisbon, where she met Abe Hanratty. And so it goes, hard beginnings: girls by necessity turned out of their own homes, deprived of schooling, and working as servants for other families. My grandmother and her mother both worked hard, and had no expectations of deserving special treatment. The same could be said for my French great-grandmother Josephine Denny. This describes my mother Gladys's expectation as well; no one would ever have said she was "entitled." As children these women were short on mothering, they worked hard all their lives. This deprivation was my mother's legacy and mine. It partly accounts for how my mother parented my brother and me.

In the first years of marriage, Glad's mother Minnie lost so much weight from lack of food that her wedding ring fell from her finger. Six months after the marriage, the first child, Leona, was born, and my mother three years later in 1907 after a stillborn boy in 1906. Six pregnancies followed, and of those, three children survived. My grandmother, according to my mother, was severe and humorless as a young mother: she was worn out with her babies, her pregnancies, house- and store-keeping.

By 1913 Edward and Minnie Ward had started to sell groceries, almost by accident. The story goes that the aroma of Minnie's fresh-baked bread wafted down the street, and occasionally a neighbor asked to buy a loaf. Soon the young Wards were selling her bread, and groceries as well, out of their front room. They moved, setting up a store on one side of a small house on Lake Street; the family lived on the other side of the house. The store sign, inside tipped against the front window, said *Ward's Groceries*. As a girl my mother reached her arm into the pickle barrel to pull up pickles for customers.

Their last child, my Aunt Mary Carmen, born in 1925, took me to Lake

Once the Ward store and home, Ogdensburg, 2010.

A Ward baby inside the little store, undated.

The Wards' first automobile, a 1909 Ford Model T.
Baby Wesley, Edward Ward, Minnie, son Edward, Leona, and Gladys, 1914.

Ed Jr., Leona, baby Wesley, and on right Gladys, with Oswagatchie River in background, 1916.

Street on a trip I made to the north country some years ago, and I took a photo of what was once the Ward store and home.

The store did well—Edward Ward liked people and believed in good customer service—and over time the Wards were able to afford indoor plumbing, a telephone, and a used automobile. Eventually Edward's mother, stepfather, and their children, his mother's parents, and his aunts, all French speakers, moved to Lake Street to be near their successful relative.

Looking with me at the photograph of her family in the Model T, my mother remembered being in the backseat and wearing that broad hat. She said: "I think I had autistic traits. . . . I shied away from people and was very silent." Another photo along the side of the Lake Street store shows four Ward children.

As a young teen Gladys Ward broke her leg. Immobile for many weeks, she gained a great deal of weight. In my mother's high school yearbook I found a supposedly humorous item about how impossible it was for Gladys Ward to fit into the seat at her desk. How that must have stung—one among many jibes and slights she experienced. For most of the rest of her life, she remained overweight. Very self-conscious about her size, Glad went on many diets as an adult but always regained the pounds lost. Her relation to her body and what she learned to make of herself over time are part of her story. Two photographs show Glad wearing her ever-present glasses and carrying her extra weight, just about the time she graduated from high school.

Glad with siblings Paul and Mary Carmen and her father.

Glad at nineteen, 1926.

Glad's father, Edward Ward, was the grandparent I never knew. I had thought he was just a proprietor of a small grocery in a poor neighborhood of day laborers and seamstresses. But, no, I have learned from one seven-page letter of his passed on to me that there was much more to him.

Edward Ward's philosophy was that you saved half of what you earned and then you invested those savings in new ventures. He wrote often to his brother-in-law, and the one letter I have, from 1930, captures an enterprising nature. *I work a few hours each week on that building I moved, once in a while six or seven hours a day. About the gas station, off that piece of land New York Ave., the corner was vacant and I do not intend to build for a while. I also have an old barn I am going to move off Jefferson Ave. and use with two gas pumps, making a small store and drive-in gas station, leasing it, making income without too much outlay.*

Over the years Edward Ward bought seventeen low-rent residential properties, and eventually, in addition to those and the Lake Street store, he owned and leased two gas stations on main roads into town. The Wards raised their family of seven out of poverty during the Great Depression, similar to the rise Martin Dunn accomplished for his family of four, though the Wards were by no means as comfortably off as the Dunns. By the mid-1930s, with their three eldest offspring grown and on their own, Edward and Minnie had moved to a house in a better part of town; from its front yard you could see the Saint Lawrence River and Canada. Edward, ever entrepreneurial, chose a location on a busy road and installed a gasoline pump and a lunch counter on the property for additional income. That house was my first home.

My grandfather's letter gives me a vivid sense of his life and mind. He mentioned movies he and Minnie had seen, *Sunnyside Up* and *Hollywood Review*; books he'd just read, Kermit Roosevelt's *War in the Garden of Eden*, about Mesopotamia; and a biography of Elbert D. Hubbard, whom he described as *a writer, poet, free thinker, farmer, successful businessman, lover of horses in a horsey town, publisher of two small magazines and numbers of books and a binder of books of quality, founder of a very peculiar and successful artisan community in Aurora, N.Y.*

His letter went on: *You know, I used to take a grocer's monthly. It was a great grocer's monthly for a guy that was not a grocer. After reading it, I would be mad, crazy, discouraged, sick and upset because all I could do was make money and not do all the fancy things it tells about, and the time you have to read is when business is slack. Oh boy, after all there is only one good recipe for getting on easy street—to work, work and sacrifice all to get a start.* He talks about his desire to travel west that summer, and ends with: *I believe I was originally intended for a hobo kicking a tin can around the world. I have a little ache for it. All I need is the bleary blue eyes.*

I love the spirit in this letter. Edward Ward expressed more feeling, connection with people, more joy in life, more interests and energetic undertakings, more hopeful plans for the future in this one letter than what I read in the thirty or so beautifully penned letters and long journal entries my father wrote during the war.

Glad grew up seeing her father work and act in the world, wait on customers, deliver groceries to farm families miles from town, fix up and move buildings, buy property and arrange leases. And he was a family man, who enjoyed his five children, taking them for jaunts in the Ford, for picnics with scores of relatives, to the movies. Edward Ward, I believe, is the key to my mother's interior richness, her capacity to feel for others, her emotional depth. Importantly, this generous, industrious, supportive man was Gladys Ward's model of manhood; she simply, unconsciously, would expect a like goodness in other men.

Edward Ward, who had gone only through eighth grade, wanted his children to go on to higher education, and they all did. Glad's older sister, Leona, graduated from nursing school, Edward Jr. went to Clarkson, Paul would graduate from Tusculum and Mary Carmen from the Pratt Institute. He encouraged his quiet, overweight daughter, Glady, to aim high. She won the English prize in high school, and in the fall of 1926 went off to St. Lawrence University in nearby Canton, the first in the family to go to college. She would live in a boarding house, where she missed her bustling family; she had few clothes and no friends in town. Shy, overweight, ill-dressed, wearing glasses, she must have summoned such inner resources each day, and her father's belief in her was always the wind at her back.

12: The Education of Gladys Ward

Gladys Ward wanted to be a writer, but, she told me, a tweedy pipe-smoking English professor at St. Lawrence made fun of her work in front of the class her first semester. Humiliated, she turned from writing, and her dream of journalism, to science. After only two years at St. Lawrence and a ten-week premed course at Cornell University, she was admitted to the Women's Medical College of Pennsylvania in September 1929.

Why medical school? Did she want to one-up her older sister Leona, who had become a nurse? No, I believe what she told me once: her beloved brother Wesley had suffered terribly and died of kidney disease at eight years of age, when Glad was thirteen, and this deep loss was why she turned to medicine. She had witnessed the family doctor tend to Wesley, then to their mother when she lost infant John the next year, and to her little sister Mary Carmen, who later came down with a severe illness. Glad was inspired by this family doctor. Edward Ward promised to support Glad through medical school, and she was well aware of the scrimping and doing without at home that would make this possible. The Wards drove her to Philadelphia, and her mother photographed her near the school; written on the back of the photo, in my mother's hand: "Landed in Philly."

Thirty-five women entered Gladys Ward's class at the only all-women's medical college in the country. In 1929, admissions to US medical schools numbered 7,030, and of these, 4 percent were women, 312, and Glad was one. Among her classmates were graduates of Vassar, Mount Holyoke, Cornell, and Stanford. Glad and six of her classmates, however, had not earned undergraduate degrees; this was an era when entry requirements for medical school had not been standardized. My sense is that most of her classmates were from educated, affluent middle- and upper-middle-class families, whereas Glad was

Glad about to enter medical school, fall 1929.

from an uneducated working-class family, and grew up in an extremely modest house with few books, no piano, and relatives next door speaking Canadian French. She herself had worked in the Ward grocery store from the age of ten. Her father had a seamstress make a suit for her, out of durable blue serge, and that was her best outfit for four years. I wonder how many of her class-mates sewed their own underwear, as Glad did, out of cotton flour sacking, a frugality practiced during the Depression. Some days Glad had to decide whether to spend her last nickel on a tram to take her the several miles from her boarding house to class, or to buy a donut to eat for breakfast and lunch. Raised as Roman Catholic, she attended Mass regularly in Philadelphia, until one Sunday when the priest denigrated those who could not put money in the offering plate. She turned her back on the Church forever.

Gladys Ward often felt clueless in her classes. For example, a professor used the term medulla oblongata—she had never heard of it, didn't know how to spell it, or where it was. Advanced chemistry, anatomy, dissection . . . the coursework and labs were a huge challenge for her. Seven students in the class of '33 dropped out, and I was told by an archivist at Drexel University, which now houses WMCP academic records, that the school had put Glad on probation for two quarters. She always told me that doggedness, not bril-liance, got her through the four years of medical school. She said becoming Dr. Ward was the proudest moment in her life, that no one could take that away from her.

Dr. Gladys Ward, 1933.

Celebrating graduation with parents and sister Leona.

Glad with Mary Niemeyer (left) and other friends, 1933.

During her four years in Philadelphia, Glad made good female friends. Mary Niemeyer, a native Philadelphian, an art student, was mistaken for Glad several times (both young women were largish, both dark-haired) and finally they met and became fast friends. Glad was an attendant at Mary's wedding, they exchanged Christmas cards all their lives, and spent time together in their late sixties, both widows. Glad's smile is so genuine in the photo of her with Mary and friends. I sense that she is very happy and can really be herself with her pals.

Graveyard Shift in the Bronx

The next step in Glad's career path, finding an internship, proved discouraging for the new physician. Owing to both the prejudice against women by the all-male medical establishment and the constrictions of the Great Depression, Dr. Gladys Ward was unable to secure a training internship at any of the many hospitals to which she applied. The only position she could find was volunteer ambulance duty from midnight to 8:00 a.m.—the graveyard shift—at Fordham City Hospital in the Bronx. Instead of interning under the close supervision and mentoring of experienced physicians, she was on her own, using her medical school training as she went out every night to neighborhoods all over the Bronx. As I heard the story, the three graveyard-shift slots were designated for minorities: a female, an African American, and a Jew.

Dr. Ward, twenty-eight years old, stepped up into the rear of a Fordham ambulance with another intern. Each carried a heavy leather doctor's bag packed with instruments and supplies. Glad dealt with all kinds of emergencies: heart attacks, domestic abuse, serious household accidents. She told me of going up flight after flight of stairs and delivering her first baby; the joyful parents named their new daughter Gladys. Since this work was unpaid, Glad's parents in Ogdensburg supplied her with pocket money. For the entire year she was fortunate to be able to economize on living expenses: she bunked in with sister Leona, who was living on West 98th Street in Manhattan, supporting herself by private nursing. Glad walked the three or so miles from the Bronx to Leona's every morning at the end of her night shift.

Falling in love was the one remarkable outcome of her year in the Bronx. Glad and a fellow Fordham intern, let's call him Max Klein, fell in love. I suppose they did a lot of talking and got to know each other very well as they rode through the Bronx at night in the back of an ambulance. When Glad went home to Ogdensburg for a few weeks, Max wrote her letters on long yellow lined sheets of paper, so said my aunt, a witness then at nine years old. My mother told me that Max proposed marriage, but with a heavy heart she refused him because she knew he would suffer—his observant family would disown him if he married a non-Jew. My mother told me that he was married by 1940 and eventually settled in Connecticut, practicing medicine and raising a family. Glad kept one photo of Max. His letters are lost.

In the mid-1950s, my mother told me, they managed to meet briefly in New York City when she was taking courses there, and he gave her a charm for her bracelet. The charm was a tiny gold envelope you could open and extract a gold "note" engraved *I love you*. I believe that Max was the true love of her life.

Glad was a realist and she was practical. Expulsion from family was too great a burden for a marriage and a love to bear, she believed. She knew what her family meant to her; she could not imagine giving them up, and she refused to consider Max breaking with his family. Glad's decision to not marry Max reveals the empathy of her character, her wisdom in looking at the larger picture, and her courage in the face of heartache. No other men were in her life for a long while.

*Max and Glad, Fordham
interns, 1934.*

A Real Internship and a Residency

After that year of ambulance duty, in July 1934 Gladys started a traditional year-long internship in a city hospital in Williamsport, Pennsylvania. It's likely that a professor at her medical school, also in Pennsylvania, helped her find this post. A photograph in the Williamsport newspaper announcing the new crew of interns clearly displays the white male domination of medicine. Of the eleven interns, Glad is the one woman, and the other individual, also called out by the photo caption, is a dark-skinned male doctor from India, whose plan, it was noted, was to return to his native land to practice.

At Williamsport Hospital Glad plunged into intensive ten-week rotations in various specialties: general medicine, obstetrics, surgery, labs, accidents, and anesthesia. Another, the pediatrics rotation, was the longest, twelve weeks, and her reaction to it surprised Glad. Primarily because of her brother Wesley's death, Glad had imagined that pediatrics was the specialty for her. But when she approached a child on the pediatrics ward, the child often cried, not because of Glad but because of sickness or pain; and the crying, the suffering of

*Williamsport Hospital
interns, August 1934.*

the child, was intolerable to her. Glad decided her temperament was not suited to pediatrics. She had earned a certificate in surgery, but that hospital-centered specialty was the closed domain of men in her day. She was looking for a discipline that suited her, where she could find acceptance.

Glad had heard only a few lectures on psychiatry in medical school. Yet summers home in Ogdensburg during medical school she had worked doing research at St. Lawrence State Hospital. Now Glad learned that one of her medical school classmates was interning in psychiatry at Hudson River State Hospital in Poughkeepsie, New York. There was another internship open, which today probably would be called a residency. In 1935 psychiatry was a comparatively new and developing specialty. As a less established, perhaps less lucrative specialty, the door of opportunity opened wider for women. Glad would work at Hudson River for six years, learning psychiatry on the job at this state facility for the mentally ill. She started at an annual salary of $1,800. Like almost all employees, from the superintendent to other doctors, nurses, attendants, and groundskeepers, she lived on the hospital grounds, so that Hudson River State Hospital became her home.

Glad and Women in Medicine in the 1930s and 1940s

I wanted to better understand the historical and social context of Glad's career in medicine, as I sensed she and other female physicians faced and overcame many obstacles. Glad's alma mater, the Women's Medical College of Pennsylvania, opening in 1850, was the first women's medical college in the world. Its male founder started the school in tribute to his sister, who, he believed, could have become a physician if given the opportunity. WMCP, and the other all-women schools established after it in the late nineteenth century, filled a need because of the extreme difficulty women experienced gaining admission to medical schools in America. Interestingly, throughout its existence WMCP admitted a global array of students who often were the first female doctors in their countries. Its admission policy seems to have been free of racial prejudice; one of Glad's classmates was a Japanese American, later incarcerated in a US internment camp during World War II, who became a beloved obstetrician in San Francisco, delivering over a thousand babies in her long career. WMCP was the only women's medical school that survived into the mid-twentieth century, owing to a national shift to the authority and funding of medical schools associated with universities.

It's useful to remember that women acquired the vote in the United States only in 1920, when Glad was thirteen years old. She went off to medical school nine years later. In the early 1900s the president of the Oregon State Medical Society claimed that hard study took away the beauty of women, brought on hysteria, neurasthenia, dyspepsia, astigmatism, and dysmenorrhea. He lectured that educated women could not bear children with ease because study arrested development of the pelvis, enlarged the fetus's head, and resulted in a childbirth of extensive suffering. Glad never read or heard these statements, of course, but she most probably was exposed to the notion that women were not suited to serious intellectual endeavor. The importance of Glad having a father who always urged her to reach higher cannot be overestimated. I do not know the story of how Glad learned about WMCP, but it provided four years among women of intelligence and sense of purpose, as well as a network useful for the future. For the shy, introverted young woman she was, a women's medical school was perhaps the best environment for her to succeed.

Once graduated from medical school, Gladys Ward MD entered the medical profession, which comprised 94 percent men, with virtually none of the remaining 6 percent women in positions of authority. Female physicians were barred from membership in many medical societies, even barred from hospitals. Did Glad present a problem to Williamsport Hospital in 1935 as the only female intern? Interns worked long shifts, sometimes eighteen hours, and napped on premises: where would the sole female intern sleep? Would she be allowed into the doctors' lounge, once an all-male sanctum? I imagine how lonely she must have felt. So another aspect of women in medicine in the 1930s was isolation, and in addition, one can infer, lack of female role modeling and mentorship.

Once Glad determined to pursue psychiatry, she actually had moved toward a specialty where female doctors had been accepted for nearly a century. In the nineteenth and early twentieth centuries, almost all psychiatry was practiced in asylums (later renamed state hospitals) with large populations of both male and female patients. Female physicians were thought appropriate to attend to the female patient population, especially owing to mores of modesty—female doctors could attend to gynecological needs. Indeed, Glad's listing of her duties at Hudson River State Hospital in 1937 included performing gynecological exams. Once on staff at Hudson River, she was one of only two female physicians of a total of twenty-three MD's—a continuation of professional isolation and lack of mentoring by senior female role models. She would never have thought of herself as a pioneer, but I do believe she was very conscious of needing to stand up for herself, stoically pressing on in her career.

I cannot recall any instance where my mother described, let alone complained, about discrimination in her career. I don't think this is because discrimination did not exist. I can see that it happened time and again. But for Glad, her interior story detailed how very far she had come, not the many ways she had been thwarted. Her father's hero had been Horatio Alger, who wrote stories about boys who escaped poverty through hard work and honesty. Glad was heir to her father's ideal and disposition.

A Daughter's Advice

In 1936 Glad's father, Edward Ward, was in failing health at age fifty, with high blood pressure and fatigue. In the autumn he divested his business holdings, all those low-rent properties and the two gas stations, and he made plans with his wife Minnie to travel, for the first time in his life. In January 1937 in a new Chevy and a camper outfitted with bedding and a woodstove, they set off for Mexico, leaving the two youngest children, fifteen and twelve, with a housekeeper. Minnie wrote to Glad and Leona from the road: "I'll tell you it took courage [to go away] but I hope the change will be good for all of us."

Minnie kept a diary of the trip, describing travelers they met at campsites along the way and finally the colors and tastes of Mexico City and Acapulco.

Edward relished driving as far as he could each day, but he experienced hours-long bouts of coughing at night. His breathing became terribly labored and he grew weaker. They hired a driver to get back to the United States, and on March 3 Edward died in a Laredo, Texas, hospital. Minnie came home by train with his body.

I came upon a six-page letter that Glad, then thirty years old, working at Hudson River State Hospital, wrote her grief-stricken mother, with advice about money and living on her own. Minnie Hanratty Ward knew nothing of finances, of how to drive a car, or of living independently without a husband; and she was now solely responsible for the two children at home. The next ten years would be the hardest financially, Glad wrote, and advised her mother not to tie up the insurance money, but to have it easily available. Her own income would increase in the next few years, she said, and she would do her part to help with the education of her brother and sister. But her letter goes on to offer so much more than practical advice. It reveals Glad's depths of empathy, her practicality, and her generosity.

Glad had lived far from home, she had been lonely, she made do with little money. Of course she, too, had lost Edward Ward. And she had given up Max, whom she loved. Glad arrived at advice for her mother through her own experiences.

That this letter survives somehow seems remarkable to me. I suspect it still exists because my grandmother treasured it. Written on both sides of three sheets of yellow lined paper, its fountain pen ink is now red. I read and am deeply moved: I look through a window into my mother's compassionate mind.

Dear Mother,

. . . Keep up with Mary Carmen and Paul. It would be easy to slump, to grow disinterested in your person and looks and just work and slave and save, and to feel justified in doing so. However that is just an escape really. It's much harder to grow interested in other people's problems, to look nice and smell sweet and smile, when you think there is no one to appreciate your doing so. . . . To gamble on yourself. 'I'll give myself this happiness now' (even if it is just owning a new dress, or spending the last nickel in your purse on a manicure). . . . In other words, live! Forget the shell you can crawl into which will protect you. Even in a shell one has to crawl out for food now and then. Living hurts! But in going through life with an anesthetized soul you miss a few of the thorns perhaps but all of the roses too. It is much better to feel the hurts, treat them with

an ointment balm and pick the roses.

Learn to enjoy your independence. It's something you've never had. Treat it as a gift, never look upon it as something forced upon you. Get joy from it. Look at it unassociated with other events. Prize it and it in turn will do things for you. It will be a steadying influence, will help you make decisions, bolster your ego, provide a sense of satisfaction. Make mistakes and never regret them. Use them. If they are costly, put that down to the cost of education.

Use even your sorrow. Let it make you more understanding of other people's sorrows. Let it give depth to your understanding. Don't become absorbed by it. Become broader rather than narrower, by it.

Live each day graciously. Accept invitations. Accept favors as you would gifts. Let Mrs. Kelly be kind to you, let Mrs. Burley do things for you. In doing so, others get a sense of satisfaction by and from giving, it's their attempt to expand. Then do your utmost to return, in some way, the consideration shown you.

You now consider yourself merely a reflection of someone else's life. You are floundering, trying to guide yourself or get a focus from something that isn't there. Don't do that. Develop your own personality, make yourself into a person, try your own wings! Consider yourself. Consult your own desires. Do what satisfies you and don't waste thought on what others with smaller minds and narrower souls say. Know that you are right, that your conscience isn't squirming, then go ahead. Never be afraid to be wrong, if your attitude and approach are right.

Dad was a man with a broad understanding and a generosity that sprung from his very being. He wasn't shown it at home, he didn't learn it at school. It was him. Qualities that he developed. He stopped living, and we would be but poor creatures if we allowed that fact to impede us. He was productive. Don't let us be degenerative. Accept what is and go on from there. Be progressive. Don't stand still!

Live comfortably, and if you need more, we'll do our part. . . . Love, Gladdy

Before I say more about this letter and what I hear in it, I want to follow the next years for Glad's widowed mother, Minnie Ward, who did cultivate herself and her independence. At fifty she learned to drive a car. For income, she turned her home on Ogden Street into a travelers' boarding house, which today we would call a bed-and-breakfast. Gram told me that an FBI agent, boarding in the early 1940s, saw my mother's medical diploma framed in the dining room and said: "Dr. Ward is *your* daughter, Mrs. Ward? She treated my mother at Hudson River and helped her a lot." She insisted on being called Mildred, not Minnie any longer. She baked, she gardened—both flowers and

Banana bread recipe.

vegetables—took photographs, and she joined the local Girl Scout leadership council. She saw her youngest two children graduate from college. Seven years after Edward's death, she married a retired Canadian railroad conductor named Will Shaffer. Will kept his home across the river in Canada and she hers.

When I began to know my grandmother on our family's summer visits, she was Gram Shaffer. An Irish storyteller, she told tales about our family that I listened to with great interest. We baked bread together. She and I wrote letters all through my adolescence and college years, and I visited her one last time before I left to live in Europe: we picnicked with my Aunt Mary Carmen, then in her midforties, in a cemetery where Gram's mother was buried. Every time I bake banana bread I go to the shelf in my study to retrieve my framed photo of that picnic and Gram's recipe, which I found among my mother's things: "Try this Glady, it's so good, easy to do and good for days."

This slip of a country girl, who loved school but went only through second grade, who worked for years as a servant: she was a match for the self-starter Edward Ward. She helped him achieve his business successes (my Aunt Mary Carmen once said, "Dad had the ideas but Mom saw them through"), and they both were passionate about their children's education. In the 1960s Mildred Ward Shaffer wrote Glad about the first family funeral in many years and remarked: "This past week most of the Ward family was home at one time, and I saw what changes education and culture have brought." Gladys Ward had two stalwart parents rooting for her in her journey.

Now, I return to my thoughts about my mother's 1937 letter to her mother. When I read that letter I hear my mother's voice. The letter reads the way my mother talked—very naturally, gently, thoughtfully. Her voice was measured, modulated. She spoke softly yet surely, and everyone in a room would stop to listen. You can actually imagine her as the psychotherapist she was becoming, as she describes how her mother will likely react to her grief (slump, slave); then she develops an array of easy, alternative, hopeful steps to bring her mother into a new state of mind, another way of approaching her life. The letter is valuable not only for how effective it was in helping Mildred Ward to take hold of her own life, but also for what it tells us about Glad—her powers of observation, her empathy, her ability to communicate.

Across the years my mother tells me even more in this letter. She reveals the attitude she brought to adversity, loss, grief, and even disappointment in her own life. For her, setbacks in life, obstacles, and emotional challenges could spur development, could deepen and broaden one's life and offer new opportunities. I believe she shared this frame of mind, this resilience, with her father. It helps explain to me how she overcame her background, her being overweight, her shyness, and many difficulties she faced in life.

The tone in this letter is also very familiar to me because my mother gave me advice in this way, advice that lifted my eyes from the ground on which I was focused up toward the horizon. So, I ask myself: how did this kind woman, who had her own form of wisdom, who was in training in psychology and, obviously, had an aptitude for it, how did she not "read" correctly the man she would soon meet?

13: Meeting Her Fate

Two years after her father's death, Gladys Ward met Gilbert Dunn.

Gil Dunn, 1939.

After completing a two-year residency in psychiatry at Hudson River State Hospital, Dr. Ward was invited to join its staff as assistant physician earning $2,200 a year. Glad had let her sister Leona know of a teaching position open at Hudson River's nursing school, which Leona promptly filled. And it was through her gregarious and very social sister that, as I described earlier, Glad eventually met Gil Dunn.

Gil Dunn was attractive and single. He seemed charming, and at the same time contained. What followed their introduction were occasional evenings of bridge with friends, a Saturday afternoon on the golf links . . . Glad did not know what Gil Dunn did for work, but he dressed extremely well and always had money. Because of Glad's intense work schedule they saw each other infrequently, and it's likely Glad assumed he was seeing other women, as I now know he was. And I also must remind myself that Glad really had very limited experience with men. There was Max, years earlier, but no one since then.

She was immersed in her profession. At Hudson River she was responsible for giving mental and physical exams, directing insulin therapy, running a community clinic, teaching, and performing both psychiatric and medical treatments. She put in long days and was assigned on many weekends to twenty-four-hour on-call duty. In her limited free time she enjoyed Gil's company, but she didn't contemplate his life story. She was predisposed to believe the best about him because her model of a man was her industrious, generous, supportive father. What she didn't know about Gil, she filled with positives—that was her default position. When Gil invited her to meet his family in Mahopac, she sensed that Gil was showing her off and this pleased her greatly. He seemed most gentlemanly to Glad, and actually he kept his distance physically.

How would I describe Gladys Ward? Introverted, hardworking, responsible, and deeply connected to her family. Part of her salary went toward saving for the educations of Paul and Mary Carmen, just as she had assured her mother. Glad had studied how her friends, especially Mary Niemeyer, dressed, how they set an attractive dinner table, and how they furnished their apartments. She learned late how to groom herself, her hair, her nails, since she came from people who had no luxuries, for whom the idea of style had no relevance. Over the years she transformed herself—from a frumpy, impecunious medical student to a sophisticated-looking professional woman.

For the first time in her life, she was able to afford nice items of clothing,

Glad, medical student, with sister   *Dr. Gladys Ward, 1942.*
Mary Carmen, 1932.

a black seal coat she loved, feminine blouses to go with her work suits, more than one pair of shoes, a fashionable leather handbag and gloves.

And somewhere in these years she began to smoke cigarettes. Smoking was advertised in newspapers and magazines and on the radio as modern and sophisticated. How many films of the thirties and forties showed a glamorous woman whose cigarette was lit by Clark Gable or William Powell? Smoking for Glad became an hourly calming ritual: her Ronson silver lighter flicked open to flame, the crystal ashtray, the inhale, smoke curling in the air, and her finger delicately dabbing a speck of tobacco off her tongue. This was a habit she would share with Gil, who'd been smoking since his midteens.

In December 1940, a year and a half after meeting Gil Dunn, Gladys Ward learned he had enlisted in the Army Air Corps. Since the midthirties, the newspapers and radio had described in detail the turmoil in Europe, then the invasions and declarations of war. Enlistment was patriotic and manly, a step Glad was sure to understand, even admire. Gil left for an airfield on Long Island. In the following two years while Gil was in training and stationed stateside, Glad saw him the few times he was on leave visiting his parents. He wrote Glad occasional postcards—she saved six, all brief and friendly.

In fall of 1942 Dr. Gladys Ward was offered and accepted the position of senior psychiatrist at an elite private institution: New York Hospital—Westchester Division, sited on a 217-acre campus in White Plains, New York. Without expecting it, or aiming toward it, Gladys Ward, who grew up on Lake Street in Ogdensburg, was now on staff at one of the country's top private psychiatric hospitals. Professionally, she had truly arrived. After living six years at Hudson River State Hospital in Poughkeepsie in a single room in a dormitory, she now moved into a spacious, well-appointed two-bedroom staff apartment—the very first apartment of her own—which was part of her compensation.

Her new employer—this branch of New York Hospital at the time was also called Bloomingdales (for the road it was on)—was exceptionally well staffed and well equipped, and was a leader in the latest psychiatric treatments. Some of Glad's patients were in motion pictures, in finance, and from high society. I remember a few names. She was to be fully engaged and happy in her work there. Again, she made a few good female friends, and with visits home to Ogdensburg she stayed close to her mother and other family, including brother Ed Jr., who now had two children. But she yearned for a family of her own, as she watched her brother with his son Edward and his daughter Carol Ann. For years she had put aside this desire, but it kept emerging, surprising her again and again.

Here is another time in this journey where I make a leap based on strands I have pulled together. The leap concerns the agency that turned the acquaintanceship of Gladys Ward and Gilbert Dunn into a relationship. How well had they known each other from their meeting in summer 1939 to his departure for North Africa in October 1942? I wondered: in those three years had Gladys Ward ever even spent a whole day with Gilbert Dunn? What moved these two people closer?

In fall 1942 this man was shipping out overseas to war, this man who perhaps was Gladys Ward's best chance at having a husband and children—if he survived. It seems to me that at the precipice of Gil's departure for war, Glad declared herself. She offered to write him, to consider him special, to be exclusive. I believe that Glad took the initiative. In his first letter to her from Africa in early November he wrote for the first time, *Hello "Darling"*—yes, with those perhaps reluctant quotation marks—and he ended the letter simply with *Gil*. In her December 1942 Christmas note to Gil overseas, the only early piece of her correspondence that still exits, she had closed with *All My Love, Glady*. It was a full four months later, in April 1943, before Gil signed off *Love, Gil*. To me it's clear that Glad took the lead crafting a relationship, took the lead in loving.

Imperatives of Body and Soul
White Plains, December 1942

In the small market
where she buys cigarettes
she sees a toddler,
golden ringlets
like the Ward babies,
all the siblings she adored
and mothered.
Her throat spirals tight.
Unbearable wet globules
blur the world. She wills
not to blink, absorbs
grief back in. She stills
herself, grabs matches
on the way out.

Every few months:
suddenly a child
seizes her heart.
She is shocked
at her huge feelings.
She buries longing

in long hours of work,
but every month
her period comes.
She writes her soldier
overseas. Will he
make it home? Does he
love her? She's in
her thirty-seventh year.
War and time
are her enemies.
She will fight
her damnedest.

Below are images Glad and Gil chose to keep near. Glad pasted the snapshot of Gil on the inside front cover of the album she purchased to display his postcards from overseas. As for Gil, he carried the tinted portrait of Glad around the world in a small leather frame. Did she give this to him on the fall day in 1942 when I suspect they made a pact to write each other? Before she even knew he spelled his name Gil, not Gill?

Images to dream on during World War II.

Over the next year and a half Glad would sit in her comfortable chair in her living room on the hospital campus in White Plains and write Gil letters on onionskin stationery. She read between the lines in his letters, and compared the gleanings with what she read of battles reported in the newspapers; she imagined what he couldn't say, wouldn't say. Occasionally she wrote about her world. In one of only three letters of hers that were saved from her wartime correspondence, she wrote: *I've done a two day stretch with only four hours sleep, since I stayed up last night working up a case, doing midnight rounds and trying to prevent a girl from doing a nose dive back into an extremely bad state which she seems to like better than reality.* Most of the time, however, she kept her subjects on the light side—how many trees on the hospital grounds had been felled by a freak windstorm (forty-five), the latest fashion in footwear (toeless high heels), the rose-red shade of her latest nail polish, a sample of which she painted in the margin of her letter.

I felt there was something I was not seeing in this wartime correspondence. I decided to not simply reread all my father's letters again, extracting each, again, from its envelope, admiring his handwriting, stopping for a cup of tea . . . but, instead, at my laptop I would transcribe them to create one long document. I suspected that reading his correspondence chronologically as a whole might reveal a pattern that otherwise had escaped me. And that happened. I discovered that Glad led their correspondence. Because so few of her letters remained, it was how Gil responded to her that allowed me to see that she was leading and Gil following, often with his apologies.

Just received your letter, Gil wrote, *in which I was very properly reprimanded. Your subtle manner was very amusing and yet I felt quite sorry for what appeared as utter neglect on my part. I know this is war from the evidence hereabouts, but your surprise move took me unawares and it appeared as though you were opening another front, back in White Plains.* Her move was to threaten not to write to him, because he ended this letter with: *May I quote, not to mimic, but just for fun: "This letter, my dear, constitutes my last effort until I hear from you."*

Five days later he wrote: *I see you are a lady of your word. (No letters.)* Four months later, he apologized again: *Believe me when I say that I am sorry not to have written you more frequently . . .* And: *Remember, I've been called to task . . .* A few months later, he followed her lead: *I have before me your letter of October 3rd. So as I peruse it again, I shall ramble along, much the same as you did.* His January 1944 letter included: *So, you like to pitch a little hell my way from time to time, eh? How unladylike.*

One "incident in letters" between the two of them is harder to decipher, but it is one in which, again, Gil apologizes. *Frankly, Glad, I feel quite ashamed of my conduct in the matter past. Two wrongs do not make a right and I'm truly sorry for any discomfort I may have caused you. I had the good sense to voice my objections in full on June 18* [a missing letter] *but instead my bull-headedness, or what have you, succeeded in the delaying action, which accomplished naught and only fostered additional discontent over a longer period of time. Your letters during this period were a constant reminder of your forbearance, which I can't help but admire, but since by that time . . . my stone was cast, I awaited your ultimatum. Needless to say it hasn't come yet . . . and if it never does, I'm satisfied that I have been a chump. "Lady of Jet," forgive me—please.* Apparently Glad "forgave" him, because he wrote within two weeks: *I sincerely hope that the 'episode past' does not happen again and as the self-adjudged instigator, I'll see that it doesn't for I don't want to be that damned unhappy, I found out.*

Perhaps more important than the mysterious subject of this episode are the relative stances of Glad and Gil, again with Glad in the dominant position. Her leadership in their correspondence also supports my inference that it was she who suggested they write each other—it was she who set them on the path to become sweethearts.

Glad did get from Gil what she wanted: letters, some very long. I think of all his tender salutations—*Lamb, Chickadee, Sweet, Darling, Non-expendable One, Lady of Jet*— and how these endearments must have been like honey to her. The variety of different appellations shows a flamboyance in Gil—actually I think it was flight into super-idealizing fantasy about Glad. He calls her *Siren!* and *Babe!* In contrast, Glad writes: *Hello darling,* or *Dearest Gil.* I wonder if all the flowery, even extravagant, appellations gave Glad the psychiatrist any pause, if the almost entirely unemotional and unintrospective cast of Gil's letters gave her pause. Or was she wooed away from any such thoughts by charm and deft storytelling, and the comfort at last of having someone to love?

When after two years and three theaters of war Gil Dunn shipped home to the United States in December 1944, exhilaration flooded Glad. Here he was, in the flesh, safe. He was thin, his head almost skull-like with his weight loss and baldness, but to her he looked handsome in his uniform, and Gil greeted her with a euphoria that matched her own. It was Christmastime, then New Year's, and her heart was bursting with joy.

~

Gil and Glad impetuously decided to marry. I never learned how this came about. I know Glad wrote her mother on New Year's Eve with wedding details and described introducing Gil to her colleagues at holiday parties. *People are telling me how nice he is—as if I didn't know it. But I like to hear it. . . . We hope he'll be stationed at Mitchel Field on Long Island.* Within ten days of his return they were man and wife. Dr. Gladys Margaret Ward wed a virtual stranger, Staff Sergeant Gilbert Martin Dunn.

I think the small wedding ceremony and reception was the last time Glad's heart was truly joyful with this man. What followed was intimacy, first at her apartment, then in Atlantic City, the honeymoon my mother called "unpleasant." The longer I have contemplated this time, the likelier it seems to me that sex was not successful for them. I can imagine my mother, in her kindness, attempting to make little of her disappointment, "to bolster Gil's ego," a phrase of hers that rings in my memory. Did she, who always thought of her body as fat, at first feel at fault—that she was not attractive enough to excite him? I can imagine Gil's humiliation, shame, and enormous discomfort. How in the world did they manage those two weeks together as man and wife, first at her apartment, then in a hotel in Atlantic City?

Glad was fast developing a sense of how different Gil was from her idea of him. The intense time of the honeymoon, whole days together, could not help but show her more of his real self—sensitivity revealed as self-absorption, his emotional shallowness, his racial and ethnic prejudices. Glad could feel with her whole being that she was no longer his *Lamb*, *Siren*, or *Babe*. But I am certain she told him that her love was sure, that they needed to be patient, that all would come right with time.

Gil's departure for an Army Air Forces convalescent hospital was a complete surprise to Glad and most unsettling. She knew the primary purpose of AAF hospitals was to identify and treat emotional problems. Glad must have asked herself how much she did not know about her husband. What state of mind or behaviors did the military observe that marked Gil Dunn for a psychiatric convalescence? In the letter she sent Gil just after they parted, he for Kentucky, she back to White Plains after the honeymoon, I read again her words: *You are the most beautiful thing that ever happened to me and that anything could happen to this lovely thing is unbelievable. I love you completely, darling—and feel sure that your love for me is equally sincere, which makes things perfect.* Does her calling him a "thing" here reveal an unconscious apprehension of his emptiness? She was sure his love was "sincere" (a strange word; I would expect "deep" or "true")—but maybe she had a sixth sense that it was not sincere.

Gil had been at the hospital in Kentucky only a month when Glad received his bombshell of a letter stating that he wanted to divorce. She mustered every shred of persuasion to plead that he reconsider. Glad felt if anyone could help this man, it was she, with her psychiatric training, her empathy, and her will to make the marriage work. Glad did what she advised her mother to do—*help others and they will reciprocate . . . understand others, and you will broaden.* I wonder, though, did she let herself consider ending the marriage? She never told me. Her letters to Gil—I'm sure she must have written many—were effective. After sixteen weeks convalescing at Bowman, Gil reunited with Glad in May 1945. Again, she took the lead, she had persuaded him.

However, Glad's whole conception of Gil had undergone a revolution. She realized that she had been smitten by the handsome charmer she'd met in the late 1930s, but that charmer was not the man she was married to. And her sinking heart knew the active primary role she had played in making the romance, relationship, and marriage happen, uniting her to a person who was slowly revealing another self to her.

Over the summer of 1945 the marriage held together as he was discharged from the military; they socialized with his parents and then traveled upstate to visit Glad's mother. Glad and Gil are smiling together in several photos taken that August in Ogdensburg and, yes, I imagine they had consummated their marriage by then. If I am right, hope rose inside Glad again, hope for the possibility of a child.

However, as they settled into daily life in the fall, Glad working full-time and often weekends at New York Hospital, and Gil unemployed, their newly reknitted relationship began to fray. Where was the soldier who had called her *Darling* and *Babe*? He had disappeared. Gil did not hide his dislike of her friends and colleagues, he pushed away with distaste suppers she prepared, he shied from her touch. He was monosyllabic, he was cold. She withered under his critical eye. She could not do anything right. Where once, reading his letters from overseas, she had felt adored, she now felt hated. Glad had never lived with such overwhelming negativity. She was emotionally exhausted. And then she found out she was pregnant.

They argued, and Glad's responses usually were measured and noninflammatory owing to her mild and compassionate nature. However, it's likely she felt so wounded she could hardly think or hear straight. Did she, the psychiatrist, realize that Gil's self-hatred over his aimlessness transformed into criticism of her? Did she realize he could not allow himself to feel his failures, so he found them outside himself, in the person he lived with, the person who had "baited" him with perfumed letters? Glad was not his doctor, she was his overworked, pregnant, mortified, baffled wife, and she was too emotionally entangled to figure anything out. Glad arranged a leave of absence from New York Hospital. How could she not feel profoundly humiliated in front of her colleagues, all witnesses to a failing marriage. They had watched her marry precipitately, they saw how ragged she was, how living with Gil had changed her. She had to leave White Plains. She and the child inside her needed peace.

The Long Trip North
January 1946

She packs the black Buick to the roof,
suitcase stuffed with her suits for work,
lingerie, a box of cosmetics,
another of books, her framed diploma.
She's wrapped in tissue the two sets
of glass dessert plates, wedding gifts,
precious with their fruit motifs.
Growing inside her is the being
she will know the rest of her life.
She checks the chains on the tires,
plaid lap robe and cigarettes
on the passenger seat. He hasn't come
to say good-bye, this one-year conundrum,
husband she is leaving, man of few words,
all bitter. She slips the apartment key
under the neighbor's door. She's chosen
a weekday to depart, her colleagues

at work on the wards. Slowly
she drives by the iced trees
of this private hospital, out the gate.
She has loved working here.
The wrinkled hanky blots her cheeks.
It will take her all day,
these two hundred miles north
on hard-packed snow.
She will arrive at her mother's house in the dark.
She's run away from the mess she's made
of her hard-won life. She's run home,
adult daughter, professional woman,
to her mother, who left school at eight,
her mother with floury arms, calico apron.
Love will surround her here, and quiet,
here she will find work while the baby
grows, here she will gird herself
for the next turns in the road.

*Glad on her thirty-ninth birthday,
July 3, 1946. I was born six days later
at five pounds.*

~

Resettling herself at her mother's in Ogdensburg, Glad worked part-time at St. Lawrence State Hospital and took on at least one private patient, from a prominent manufacturing family in town. Unlike Gil, she rarely stopped working all her life. The state hospital administration, impressed with her work, offered her a full-time position, but she declined. In early July after giving birth to the child she had so much wanted, she was crying with joy in her hospital bed, she told me, and she overheard the hometown nurses gossiping, speculating that she was weeping because she was unmarried.

When in late July Gil took the train up to Ogdensburg, Glad listened to his apologies and excuses for his behavior in the fall. Returning to the person she knew before the war, his charming self, he promised to be a good husband and father.

In the Garden
July 1946

Glad overhears her mother
answer the door.
"Your wife and your daughter
are in the garden. This way."

Pink peonies are unraveling,
and the roses. The baby
sleeps in white flannel,
against her bosom.

She looks up and sees
the husband she left
seven months ago:
"This is Sharon."

She and he will reconcile.
She can see it now.

This is his child. She
doesn't believe in divorce.

But she knows his emptiness.
Here in the abundant garden
facing him, she senses the future,
the long hard last chapter.

She smooths the blonde wisp
on the infant's head. Cherish.
Protect. Love without end. She will
lay down her life for this child.

Although Glad, Gil, and infant spent nearly two months at Gram's house in Ogdensburg, only one photograph documents that time. My mother in a large patterned dressing gown holds me up with a great smile; someone standing beside her has been torn out of the photo. Was it my father? Mildred, my Gram, had become the Ward family photographer. Indeed, she had photographed Glad and her newborn with Gil's parents when they visited in mid-July, but she took only this one now-torn photo after that. How strange with a new grandchild not to take photos of both parents and child—but there are none. It makes me come to the conclusion that my grandmother had passed judgment on her son-in-law.

So Glad reunited with Gil after my birth. By November 1946 she was pregnant again and she resigned from New York Hospital. During her stay-at-home hiatus in a rented cottage in Mahopac, which lasted until Mike was nine months old, Glad enjoyed domesticity. She still managed some professional activities—she delivered a coauthored paper on involutional melancholia to the American Psychopathological Association, gave talks to at least two nursing associations on the state of psychiatry, and substituted for another doctor giving immunizations at a children's clinic. How did the household support itself, with only Gil's day jobs and a year's unemployment compensation offered all veterans?

In spring 1948 Glad returned to work full-time, as acting supervising psychiatrist at the state hospital in Wingdale, New York, a step down professionally from elite New York Hospital. This meant our family moved to

Harlem Valley State Hospital, where Dr. Dunn arranged for her children to be minded by patients who could be trusted.

Then only months later Glad's former boss, Dr. S., invited her to assume a directorship at the state mental hospital in Concord, New Hampshire. Glad was deeply pleased that Dr. S. had confidence in her. Beyond that, why did she consider this job? At Harlem Valley she was again doing routine admissions, which she had performed as an intern, and her family was living in dormitory-like quarters. In New Hampshire, Glad's title would be clinical director, she would be a member of the senior administrative staff, and she would set up and manage mental health clinics all over the state—work offering a professional challenge and growth. Her family would live in a two-story brick house with its own lawn. What about Gil? She hoped this move could be a fresh start for him but she must have worried.

In October 1948 our family set off for New England in the Buick. Trees in gold and scarlet glory lined the roads. In our new home on the hospital grounds, Mike and I shared a bedroom, each with our own crib. We were so unformed, just one and two. Mother looked forward to her new work. But for Gil, was New Hampshire a fresh start? Or did this move bring him to the edge of the abyss? Over decades this home would be the intimate stage for his struggle to feel self-worth, for my mother to hold us together while she earned a living, the stage for a bleak family drama unseen by the world outside our walls.

Mike, almost one, and me, two, with a patient, Harlem Valley State Hospital, July 1948.

14: Taking Care

O ur household was out of the ordinary: the mother of a two toddlers worked full-time as a professional supporting the family, while the father remained at home, unemployed. Who took care of us children? At first Bessie did, the patient whom Mother brought with us on "convalescent status" from Harlem Valley State Hospital. But after less than eighteen months we drove Bessie back for readmission to her hospital.

Bessie had begun thinking that we were her children—a sad delusion, and poignant too, given that we saw more of Bessie than we saw of our mother.

Mike, Bessie, and me, 1948.

My Aunt Mary Carmen only recently recalled that one night my father stationed himself in front of the bedroom Mike and I shared. I am guessing that our parents feared Bessie might—what? try to run away with us? A year after Bessie's departure Mother inquired if she could come back to us, and the hospital's reply was that Bessie had undergone electroshock treatments and was not doing well. Why did our mother inquire? I am sure she hoped Bessie's condition had significantly improved, and she knew that Mike and I had loved Bessie. Indeed, one of my earliest memories is looking out the oval back window of the black Buick and waving good-bye to her.

For a while a series of day women, hired by my father, watched us. One walked me to kindergarten and slapped my face just as we walked past a neighbor's front window; another washed out Mike's mouth with soap. These are the incidents I remember. Mother was furious when she learned months later from the neighbor about the slap; she never knew about the soap. Did she realize that when our father had to substitute and take care of us, he did the minimum of grudging caregiving, leaving us to ourselves in our room or at the sandbox?

Glad as Professional Woman, Wife, and Mother, 1940s–1960s

Gladys Ward, who had faced so many challenges as a woman in male-dominated medicine, now faced more challenges as Dr. Gladys Ward-Dunn, wife, mother, and full-time professional. In the late 1940s, and onward for decades, the career woman with young children could expect little or no help from employers, coworkers, friends, family, or husband regarding childcare. Nursery school, preschool, daycare, and flex workdays did not exist the way they do now. Thus Dr. Dunn with two children under two and a half had to rely on a trusted mental patient to care for her very young children as she took up her new job in New Hampshire.

"The postwar desire to return to 'normalcy' in the 1950s helped create a particularly conservative social climate . . . [including] an almost total rejection of feminist programs and awareness," write the authors of *The History of Women in America*. Conventional wisdom in the fifties was that the right to vote in 1920 had concluded the feminist movement—America's second wave of feminism would launch only in 1963 with Betty Friedan's *The Feminine Mystique*. I saw the stay-at-home mom idealized in 1950s TV shows: *The Adventures of Ozzie and Harriet, I Love Lucy, Father Knows Best, Leave It to Beaver*. The only programs I recall with working women were *Our Miss Brooks* and *Perry Mason*, where the career women were single. No married (or unmarried, for that matter) female doctors, lawyers, professors . . . none. As a young teen raised with these images of mothers on TV and in magazines, I too felt that home was the place for a mother. Accompanying a new friend to her house after school, I was delighted when her mother greeted us with cookies just out of the oven. I had a pang of envy, to have a mother at home.

Our family subscribed to *Life* magazine. I wonder if my mother read the December 24, 1956, issue, which described the "career woman syndrome." The career woman "may find many satisfactions in her job, but the chances are that she, her husband and her children will suffer psychological damage, and that she will be basically an unhappy woman." A woman's career, it suggested, creates illness. The opinions of five psychiatrists from around the country served as bases for the article; I'm not surprised that all five were men. In this social climate my mother breathed, lived, worked, and mothered.

Glad's medical school conducted a Women in Medicine Oral History Project, which focused on twelve graduates from the 1920s and 1930s. Those who never married all had full-time careers. Of those who married (all to physicians, by the way), none carried on full-time careers and raised children at the same time. My mother differed from all twelve—she was an outlier: she married and raised two children while conducting a full-time career; and she married a man who was not a physician.

Anna Arrives

When Gil was ready to launch his bird-feeder business in 1952, my mother felt fortunate to at last hire a live-in housekeeper, a thirty-four-year-old Latvian refugee, whom I introduced earlier. Anna Obsenieks had immigrated to the United States following her one-time employers, Dr. and Mrs. B., now living in rooms in our hospital's Main Building. Anna spoke no English and she was homesick for her country, now behind the Iron Curtain.

When friends learn I grew up with a housekeeper, they think I was lucky, cared for by a Mary Poppins. But, really, Anna was a silent servant, who worked stoically, from six in the morning, squeezing oranges for fresh juice, to evenings, ironing in the basement. Her language for Mike and me was food: we breakfasted on her raisin pancakes, we tasted warm chocolate chip cookies

Mike and Anna, 1955.

cooling on racks. Anna was a good cook and gardener, a fine baker, a good-enough cleaner, and, as for childcare, well, we were always safe.

I would know Anna the rest of her long life, long past my childhood, to a time when she actually bought her own small house in Concord at age eighty and dug a garden out back, planting vegetables and cherry trees. Of course I had grown to love her, she was like daily bread. I saw her hard work, her loneliness, her indomitable spirit.

Anna Lived with Us

She came from the countryside
of the old world where mothers
grew flax for the linen they wove,
where she herded cows, churned butter.
She could not speak our language
so she did not speak. She cooked,
cleaned, mended, ironed,
made beds, began her garden.
She lived in a room in the basement,
cinderblock painted turquoise,
asbestos-swaddled pipes overhead.

She was always in the house, except to walk
to the little market to buy a loaf of bread.
She left us alone to play indoors
and outdoors. She made sandwiches,
for lunch at the sandbox. She baked cookies,
brownies, cupcakes and we could lick
the beaters. She became the roof
over our heads, the house that held us,
the body between us when we fought.
We raced around the kitchen table
yelling and hitting, and she was mute
witness to our love.

Only when I had a child of my own and was working and needed to hire caregivers, did I reflect on the sorts of people my mother had left us with. We had been looked after by mentally ill women; hired girls who were mean; our father whom we annoyed; and finally Anna, who spoke no English at first, and never well. Nowadays, we have this tired phrase: *What was she thinking?* This phrase is spoken with dismay tinged with humor. What *was* my mother thinking? But, looking at the history of the women in her family, none had or was a model of a nurturing mother. Children were left on their own, to

*Our father exacted this
promise from Mike, 1955*

make their own way, to be watched by elder siblings, and sometimes they were farmed out to work. I think my mother believed she was doing all right by us, the best she could manage.

Our father, ever the backdrop as disciplinarian of the home, found fault with Mike and me constantly. He ordered us to our room—not for ten minutes, but for hours. As punishment for something I said, he had me write twenty-five times: *I will not be insolent to my elders.* A six-year-old, I did not know what *insolent* meant. He also exacted notes from my brother.

What brewed in me as a young child were obsessive fears, tears, and dreams connected to what I was living. In grade school, the school nurse scared me. In the darkened room she examined my eyes and ears, listened to my heart, and palpated my glands at throat and groin, and I dreaded her. Just to glimpse her, tall and thin in a dark blue uniform down the hall, turned the air cold. Maybe I really was reading someone who was not to be trusted; maybe I could sense danger because I was familiar with it. Yet I also know now that she was an amalgam of my parents. She was a female medical person (like my mother, the doctor) and her name was Miss Gilman, a name conjoining my father's name, Gil, and his gender. Here was another dangerous person, right here in school, where I longed to be safe.

All during those young years, until I was about twelve, I think, I cried myself to sleep. Every night. How could my mother not know that? Why would I not tell her? Did I think everyone cried themselves to sleep?

At the same time I had a recurring scene—was it a dream, a fantasy?—that I ran inside my head every night as I lay down. I was in an operating theater in a hospital, on the table, and cigarettes were stubbed out on my genitals. It is a fact that both our parents chain-smoked, and the air in our living room was sometimes a gray haze. I was familiar with the operating room because of several eye muscle operations I had had between ages four and six in our own state hospital's Medical and Surgical Building, which we called M&S. The most abhorrent part of those operations was the sweet, suffocating ether poured in a small metal cone for me to breathe until I was unconscious. A wretched smell. I melded my own real experience of surgical procedures with a dark fantasy of cigarettes—and smoke, which was in its own way suffocating. Both my nurse-dread and the recurrent dream have sexual components that remain mysterious to me.

I also fixated on a character in a book our mother read to us at bedtime. The book was *Golden Cat* by Alfred Bigelow Paine, with pen and ink drawings by Pelagie Doane. Young, delicate, orphaned Cathy lived with her beautiful Aunt Gerza, who was really an evil witch. When her plans were foiled by Cathy, Gerza screamed, "I'll find her and kill her! I'll turn her into a mouse and eat her alive!" I identified with Cathy but was at once fascinated and repelled by the powerful Gerza, who, like my mother, had jet black hair and wore high heels.

Both my father and my mother were represented in childhood fantasies and dreams. I think now that I dealt with the dark side, the complicity of my mother, by embedding her in those dreams, dreads, and fantasies. However, the flesh-and-blood mother I saw when she came home tired from her day's work—I yearned to nestle in her warm lap and have her brush out my hair that had been braided in long pigtails. And she wanted to hold me and hear about my day. But the mother who allowed my father to do his daily damage, who did not speak up and stop him—that mother went into my underground raging river.

Will I ever comprehend how my mother lived with my father's oppression of Mike? I can try to see the whole surround, her past, her present—the entire construction of our life, where some pieces were movable, and others simply were not. And the irony—my mother was a psychiatrist. We lived on the New Hampshire State Hospital grounds, where thousands of mentally ill patients were housed and treated. Yet our household was not healthy. It was under my father's malevolent spell, and we were in our own way sick, each of us infected by him in different ways.

15: Glad's Two Worlds

I woke my mother up every weekday at 8:00 a.m. just before I left for school. I opened her bedroom door (my father had risen much earlier), leaned over her twin bed, and gently shook her shoulder. I hated waking her. I wanted her to sleep as long as she needed to, but she had to get up for work. Invariably she was groggy because she had stayed up past 1:00 a.m. in the living room watching *The Tonight Show* with Jack Paar, and later Johnny Carson. That was her precious time alone. She half groaned, propping herself up on an elbow to look at the clock and sigh.

On Her Own: Psychiatrist and Working Mother

Most mornings a car pulled up to the front of our house, and a social worker drove my mother off to a New Hampshire city or town—Keene, Portsmouth, Dover, Manchester, Nashua, Plymouth, Berlin, or Littleton, where at daylong mental health clinics she listened and wrote prescriptions. She saw fifteen patients, sometimes more, back to back, with a half hour off for lunch. Imagine all the stories she heard, the depression and pain she saw, the schizophrenia she medicated. On nonclinic days she walked across the road to the large brick building that held her office, an admissions center, and several wards; there she dictated case notes, attended meetings with colleagues, and treated her hospitalized patients. Later in her career she was responsible for half the hospital population. She created and managed programs for alcoholics and for hospitalized young children.

〜

Working Mother

I stand over you,
touch your shoulder lightly.
Mum—it's time to get up.
As I leave for school
you are drinking coffee,
looking over lists of meetings.
A second cup cools
on the white tablecloth
next to your keys.
Today you are wearing the navy suit,
red shoes with thin heels,
earrings like red flowers,
your long nails polished perfect.

I hear heels on the sidewalk.
You are home for supper
before "evening hours"
with private patients.
Case histories of strangers
are piled on the carpet.
You go out, you come in.
I am awake, asleep.

I stand over you
and touch your shoulder lightly.
The sheets are damp with your sleep.
Today you wear a grey dress,
spectator pumps
and simulated pearls—
a necklace and bracelet
I have tried on
looking through your drawers
in the long afternoons.

Hospital fair, 1951, chatting with colleagues.

My brother and I saw so little of our mother that every occasion we were with her seemed special. When we were four and five, she brought us to the hospital Christmas pageant to portray angels, where Mary and Joseph and the three kings were patients and baby Jesus was a doll. Mike and I wore wings and halos and had to stay very still. Someone gave us an oatmeal cookie afterward, and I have never given up trying to find an oatmeal cookie that tastes as good. Every summer the nursing students ran an outdoor fair for patients; Mother took us from booth to booth proudly—we were the only children there.

Mother's job required her, and thus her family, to live on the hospital grounds. Supplied with a furnished house, my parents never needed to own furniture, appliances, linens, crockery, or tableware, or needed to pay for heat or electricity. They didn't need to mow the lawn, rake leaves, shovel snow, paint, or repair any part of the house. Our groceries, including prime meats, bread and ice cream (made by hospital kitchen staff), and milk from the hospital dairy, were delivered free twice weekly to the back door after a list of items was phoned in by my mother, and in later years by Anna. Irish cleaning women came twice a year to scour the house. The hospital was its own little world of curving roads with white curbstones and lampposts, broad lawns and shade trees, post office, movie theater, telephone operator, power plant, bakery, kitchens, laundry, grounds maintenance sheds, nurses' dorms and classrooms, greenhouse, tennis courts, miniature golf. And inside the many large red brick buildings: the many wards, and the thousands of souls, nearly twenty-five hundred in the 1950s.

Mike and I were friendly with many patients. Every day, tall, gaunt Caspar with his honey-colored cocker spaniel raised the Stars and Stripes up the flagpole on the sweeping lawn in front of the Main Building, and monthly he waxed our family car. Morris, always with skullcap, manned the linen delivery truck, hoisting the canvas hopper off the truck and dragging it into our basement. I played tennis with hospitalized teens, including Ray, a handsome sociopath, and Miriam, a schizophrenic who, when not hospitalized, was my mother's private patient.

The grounds were beautiful. In mild weather clusters of patients, with uniformed attendants, walked the roads for exercise. Patients able to be on their own relaxed in wooden garden chairs in the shade of oaks near our house: I would amble by and chat. Eight-foot-high purple lilacs bordered our way to grade school. We walked past deep beds of bearded iris, azalea, and rhododendron bushes, specimen trees of great girth, a quarter-acre garden of peonies. In winter, strings of colored lights decorated the huge fir trees, and the grounds superintendent delivered red poinsettias from the hospital hothouse to our home.

I had no fear living on the grounds, even though prison wards incarcerated the criminally insane. When as a nine-year-old I cut across the Main Building lawn on the way to school, the men behind bars called out to me: *What do you have in your lunch pail, girlie? Wish I could have some.* For the most part, though, the hospital's acres served as a playground; with the other employees' kids we roamed the secret places—Old Asylum Pond, the grassy-edged brook, the miles of fencing that separated us from the quiet streets of Concord. Mike and I climbed out on the roof of the Main Building portico and lay on its tarry shingles in the sun. Our working mother had no idea how well we knew the hospital grounds, how often we explored its alleys and fields.

In those early years my mother wore mannish suits that were the staple of professional women in the 1940s and early 1950s. She always wore high heels, bright red lipstick, and matching nail polish. She was hefty in her forties and

Glad at fifty. Others, left to right: me, full-grown at eleven, Anna, my brother in the doorway, a young cousin, and my Gram— Mildred. 1957.

fifties but with lovely erect carriage. In her early forties, her thick black hair developed a broad silvery streak above her forehead, and eventually she cut her hair very short and wore it that way the rest of her life, as it turned entirely silver and then white. She had chocolate-pudding brown eyes, a long aquiline nose with pronounced nostrils, a forehead with a horizontal indentation, and she was big boned and five foot six inches, made taller by three-inch heels. She was always dieting; her current diet—the egg diet, the grapefruit diet, the protein diet, the latest fad diet—was taped to the end of the cupboard in the kitchen, just above the month's schedule of her clinics.

By the end of the 1950s her wardrobe bloomed into dresses, skirts, and blouses, into color and pattern. I used to believe that her outfits with their strong colors and designs and scoop necks, her high heels in bright colors, the elaborate, large earrings, her necklaces and bracelets were protective armor distracting the eye from her large body. Yet today I see her way of dressing not as armor but rather as expression of her evolving taste and flair and happy escape from the deprivations of the Depression, the war, and the start-up years of my father's business. I recall her telling me with pleasure the compliments she'd gotten for her purse or earrings. Her attire inspired attention and compliments from the women she worked with. In a photo taken one morning before she was off to work, when relatives were visiting, she wore a black dress with pink flowers and a golden metal belt. To me, then and now, she seems like an Amazon.

For an introvert, and a psychiatrist to boot, her wardrobe was almost gaudy at times. She would clip on two-inch earrings made of flame-red plastic

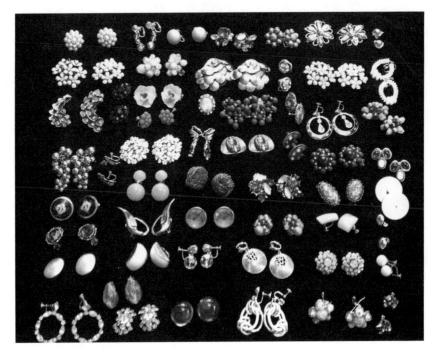

Glad's earrings to wear to work, 1950s, 1960s.

fringes and rhinestones, and as a teen I would think: You are seeing patients in those earrings? Aren't those going to disturb them? I still have a box of her costume jewelry (unfortunately those red earrings and many others were lost): this collection evokes her and her workdays for me.

Our mother had no time for our school lives or after-school activities. Of the three public schools in Concord I attended, she stepped into one only once, in first grade when I needed to go to the doctor. I don't know if she was aware that my classmates' parents did not want their daughters to go home with me because I lived on the mental hospital grounds. Somewhat socially isolated, I made friends with other hospital employees' children, two girls, who were three and four years older than I.

When we were very young our mother on winter weekends took us ice-skating and sledding on the hospital grounds. She did not skate or sled with us—I remember she wore a dress coat with nylon stockings and heeled boots with fur collars—she simply enjoyed watching us. In summer, dressed for work, she sprayed Mike and me and our Aunt Leona's daughter from a garden hose.

Mother, Mike, me, and an older cousin, summer 1954.

Perhaps my mother's biggest presence in my childhood was, paradoxically, her absence. Especially afternoons after school and evenings after dinner when she was out seeing private patients, I felt her absence. The house loomed in its quiet in the afternoons. Anna was tending her vegetable garden behind the garage, or was baking in the kitchen, and Mike had pumped off on his bike with a friend. I would enter my parents' bedroom and go to my mother's bureau, my father's highboy, and the desk, opening drawers in each, one by one. I became very familiar with all the contents: my mother's lingerie drawer with girdles, slips, and nightgowns, my father's second drawer with its two-inch stack of white cotton handkerchiefs neatly folded in squares. On the inside of the closet door hung my father's colorful abstract-patterned silk ties from the 1930s. From the shelf I took down the hatbox to look at his fedora. I leafed through every book in the small bookcase, opened the box of dominoes in the desk.

Or I occupied myself for an hour in the attic. I pulled the chain to the ceiling door in the hallway, hauled down the ladder, and climbed up. Under the rafters of the peaked roof, by the light of a dim bulb, I opened cartons of old paperwork, boxes of linens, and barrels of blankets, viewed my mother's two long evening dresses in the cedar closet, my father's flight jacket and khaki uniforms. It was hot and stuffy up there—and compelling. Both bedroom and attic held the material life of my parents, and the child I was went to these places again and again to fill an emptiness. And I'm still going back, aren't I, going back to their lives, my memories, this time constructing a story that helps me understand that emptiness.

Mother's Tongue

In our house back then
one plant lived in a corner.
The snake plant, Mother's Tongue.
Mother worked. She had no time
for plants. But this was a gift
from my father's mother,
impossible to give
or throw away.
It survived on air
and the promise of rain.
Once she snipped all its leaves
back to the soil with bandage scissors
from her doctor's bag.
But the small snakes returned
for their quarter hour of winter sun
filtered by the drapes.
I watched an oblong of light lengthen
on the carpet, touch the snake plant
and disappear. The sun slipped
behind the brick building
where she worked. The house was quiet
waiting for everyone to come home.

Several photos from different years show our mother reclined on a chaise longue in our backyard. Needing to recuperate from her week's work, she relaxed doing crossword puzzles and reading mysteries from the Detective Book Club. These photos are emblematic: our mother was often unavailable to us even in her time off. She needed to conserve her energies, restore herself on weekends so that she could perform her work well.

Mother—and Mike at age seven.

But our mother did have domestic pleasures, sudden inspirations, and spurts of energy. When Anna was off for her one weekend a month, Mother enjoyed cooking dinner—sometimes paprika stew, a recipe from Dr. Jane K., a Hungarian Jew, a camp survivor, psychologist on her staff. For a while she had a penchant for Chinese flavors, sparked by Dr. T., another refugee who worked with her. Over the years she sewed me skirts and dresses. One autumn she wanted to make Della Robbia wreaths, and we hunted in the hospital fields together for nuts and flower husks, which she sprayed gold. This was the only outdoor hike we ever had. When I was nine there was a hurricane in September, and all day Mother stayed home and cooked orange marmalade that filled the house with its sweet smell.

On some Saturdays we went shopping—this was her fun. In downtown Concord everyone at Carroll's Cut Rate knew her—she took her time perusing the latest cosmetics, the newest shades of lipstick. She purchased lingerie at the spacious Harry G. Emmons department store, where money shot by pneumatic tube to a cashier and change returned. She had a favorite store in downtown Manchester—the best for coats and good work outfits. She loved the factory outlets in the old mill buildings along the Merrimack River— where she shopped for size nine shoes on sale and Pandora sweaters for me.

Every year I embark on the Gladys Ward-Dunn Memorial Shopping Trip, probably because shopping was when I saw my mother's spirit at its lightest—out of the house, not at work, just the two of us, enjoying each other's company.

For the formal dance socials given in our town, she took pleasure in buying me beautiful dresses. But I was always the tallest and most developed female among my peers, so that wearing a sophisticated gown I looked eighteen rather than thirteen. The effort to have me fit in socially by wearing a lovely dress was obviated by how much older I looked than my classmates. Though my features and coloring came from my father's side of the family, and I looked very different from the overweight adolescent my mother had been, she and I were alike in important aspects: our interiority, our interest in how people feel and think, our love of reading.

In my college years we wrote almost weekly letters. Hers detailed her daily life, and at times she wrote what she called "lectures." Mostly she urged me to enjoy myself. I was too serious and should have fun. College was not only about academic learning but about developing all parts of one's self. I now see a link to her letter to her newly widowed mother, whom she urged to take care of herself, buy a new dress, to cultivate her new independence.

Once she asked me why I read such serious fiction—*Anna Karenina* or *For Whom the Bell Tolls*, books filled with tragedy. Every day she faced ugliness, violence, sorrow, and despair in the lives of her patients, so that she only wanted to read light fiction, mysteries, and romances. One book she read over and over was *Désirée*, a historical novel by Annemarie Selinko. Désirée Clary, daughter of a Marseilles silk merchant, fell in love with and became the fiancée of the very young Napoleon Bonaparte. Eventually she married General Jean-Baptiste Bernadotte, who later was adopted by the heirless king of Sweden. Désirée became the queen of Sweden, whose descendants are on the throne today. A young unsophisticated girl rises to a life of prominence and affluence—did my mother identify with this French girl in some way? Of course. And after a long day of listening to people's problems, she could enter this world to relax and dream.

She had no friends, really. She had colleagues and acquaintances in abundance, but no one close, no confidante. She became friendly (different from being a friend, I think) with two women, one a former patient, the other a social worker. Only a few times did she go on a jaunt with a female friend by car. One time she enjoyed a show in Boston by then outrageous comedienne

Glad and Gil's daughter, sixteen.

Phyllis Diller, who called her husband "Fang." Mother brought me home a cocktail napkin signed by Diller, and I am sure Diller's dark humor about her husband resonated with my mother. She kept her own counsel. I know she never saw a therapist herself. If she was troubled about the dysfunction in our family (and how could she not be?), her thoughts and feelings stayed inside. She saw our situation as fixed and there was no use whining. I imagine that her fear (conscious? unconscious?) was that unless mollified by her compliance, Gil would do even more damage.

In the course of her career the pharmacological revolution in the mental health field took place—dozens of new antipsychotic, antianxiety, and antidepressant drugs were developed, and Glad had to understand how they worked. That must have been a very large undertaking. In those unregulated days, all the drug companies mailed samples of their drugs to doctors, along with education materials. So trial packets of pills were always coming into our home. They piled up on Mother's side table. I self-administered a short course of Dexedrine when I read that this amphetamine would help with weight loss, and no one ever knew.

When she was in her early fifties a colleague urged Glad to establish a full-

Gladys Ward-Dunn, MD,
1966.

time private practice with him in Concord. He argued she'd earn much more as an independent psychiatrist. The lighter patient load and the opportunity to offer greater care to each individual must also have appealed to her; Glad was treating more than 250 patients a month at the clinics and on the wards. However, with the state position she had job security, a retirement plan, and housing. Private practice was financially risky, and there was already so much risk inherent in Gil's one-man business, which depended on steady income from her. So her answer was no. She daydreamed a while, though, of living in her own home, with furniture of her own, in a real neighborhood. Almost her entire adult life she had lived in an institutional setting.

Though she was called Dr. Dunn everywhere, she used Gladys Ward-Dunn MD as her offical signature. She told me she had kept the Ward name because her diploma and early medical licenses were in her maiden name. But I wonder if there wasn't another reason. As Gladys Ward she had achieved so much, and perhaps she did not want Gladys Ward to disappear.

In Gil's Orbit: Wife and Mother

Out in the world my mother acted with independence and authority, but in our house when our father was there, she became a different person. Gladys Ward-Dunn MD disappeared and a different form of her lived with us. My mother fell under my father's spell—I can't think of another way to put it. Glad was drawn into Gil's orbit early, as we all are by prospective partners. She had believed, for instance, that he really liked children. During the war when she wrote him that her sister Leona was expecting another child, he responded: "In my opinion, life's fulfillment. Think you too?" I remember her saying to me wistfully, "When I first knew him, I thought he loved children." When I unpacked that sentence's real meaning, a chill came over me.

She thought he would be generous, he would emotionally support her; and in early times, before the war, he presented this face to her, so it wasn't all her imagination. She entered the orbit of this handsome, charming man, seeing what he presented, believing what he said. And it was on this basis that she cast her lot and pursued the relationship, writing to Gil overseas, eager partner in transforming correspondence into courtship.

But after their hasty marriage, she came to know a disappointing Gil, who could be devastatingly critical, and who—it was hard to believe—for years never managed to find work. Excuse after excuse: he did not find employment that suited him, he didn't want to work with Canucks, he *might* be able to invent something. For Glad, with her own strong work ethic, her own seamless and impressive resume, what explanation can there be for her putting up with his unemployment and his excuses and not throwing him out? Perhaps voices of rationalization whispered: *I can't throw him out; he wouldn't survive—imagine him returning to Mahopac . . . imagine him devolving to poverty, or even suicide. . . . The children need a father. . . . Divorce is shameful. . . . I got myself into this marriage, I pushed him. . . . Maybe, just maybe, the business will succeed and make him successful and that will change our lives.*

Here is another possibility: Early on a tacit bargain was made—Glad would have the children she dearly wanted; and the price she would pay was—literally—to support him. Perhaps supporting him made her feel (at first?) generous and loving, even powerful? I recall the comment she made late in her life to her sister Carmen, who repeated it to me only a few years ago: "I was fortunate I could afford to support his hobby." This statement is eerie, and it shocked me, because not once in our lives together did my mother condescend about my father's business, never did she make a remark to me to indicate that it was anything but a worthy enterprise.

She handed her biweekly paycheck to Gil to deposit in the bank; so it appeared he was doing her a favor, an errand, almost. From their account he bought inventory, contracted advertising, paid rent, met all the needs of the business. And he was frugal—he had to be; there was never a lot of money, ever. When I was in college, my mother slipped a five-dollar bill in a letter to me, writing, "Daddy will kill me. He likes to keep track of things like this." She was the breadwinner! Especially when I was a teen, I hated to see her put on her coat after dinner to go across the street to see private patients. She had arrived home from an out-of-town clinic at 5:45, and an hour later she walked out the door and wouldn't be home until after 9:00. I now see how very important it was for her to have money of her own that she did not hand over to my father, worth pushing herself to work an even longer day.

Gil Dunn had found, unconsciously but like an arrow, Glad's weakness, the entry point that clenched her to him and made him superior. Despite her medical degree, experience, and independence, my mother was at her core very vulnerable, and her self-esteem was fragile. She was not confident in her body. She often tipped the scales at 185 pounds or more; she struggled to take off weight. She tried not to show her teeth when smiling because they were stained and had gaps; she had dentures at fifty. Inside her she carried all the trying times: when she was made fun of in high school, when she had no money and did not know how to dress or behave socially, or when she was in medical college and had no idea what the professor was talking about. The women in her family worked hard, they labored, and they expected to work hard for everything they got—and she was no different. She was a workhorse. Nothing came easily. She was distraught when after spending eight weeks away from us in 1955 to study at Columbia University, she failed to become "board certified" in psychiatry (a much-valued professional credential). She never said much about her failure at the orals—I heard something about her being "frozen," her words not able to come out, though she told me she knew the answers. Though uneducated, never finishing high school, Gil, trim with a strong physique, had a high intelligence and an autocratic manner. He intuited Glad's vulnerability and subtly put her down, undercut her words, ignored or belittled her wishes. Somehow, unconsciously, she expected no better. She accepted her inferiority in this most private arena. The competent self she was out in the world somehow retracted in his presence. Save us? She couldn't save herself.

That was my answer. She couldn't save us because she couldn't save herself. She had gotten herself deeply enmeshed with Gil—he fathered the children, her earnings streamed without diversion into his business, she installed him as head of the household. How long was it before she, the psychiatrist, was able to put together all her experience of Gil and diagnose him with a narcissistic personality disorder, someone with no empathy, someone who cannot change? This intellectual understanding helped her set a course: encouraging Gil to go into business for himself where he would not have to team with anyone, lowering all her own expectations, offering compliance, counseling her daughter to accept home life as it was. But this understanding resided in one part of her brain while a crippling inability to act ruled in another. Despite seeing Gil for who he was, she experienced herself as prisoner subject to his rules. There was no rebellion, no rioting, no escape. After yet another dinnertime of my father bearing down on their young son, she places her cloth napkin beside her plate; tears brimming in her eyes she leaves the room, saying only, "Oh, Gil," with a catch in her voice and nothing else.

The wretchedness was invisible. You could not point a finger at it. It confined itself to the house. Out in his world of Main Street in Penacook, local business owners, suppliers, and customers all liked Gil Dunn, thought him very personable; after his death all these folks spoke fondly of him to me. But at home, his dark eye was upon the three of us. Aunt Mary Carmen, whose family stayed with us in Concord a few times, said to me: "The atmosphere in your house was so strange, entirely unlike what I had known all my life, of Glad's warmth." My aunt was one of the few adults who entered our home for more than a few hours, who saw what went on within our walls, our secret life, contained and not talked about out in the world.

My brother was never given the advantages he could have used to develop his talents—tutoring, the military boarding school he virtually begged our mother to send him to—so he was deprived not only of better education but release from an oppressive environment. His childhood imprinted him not to react to intimate harassment. His toolkit for survival included stoicism, dissociation, and disappearance. As for me, I was shaped to accept subtly destructive behavior directed toward me; I rarely recognized it. *No* was not a word I used easily. I was too willing to give without expecting anything in return. And all my life I've struggled to recognize and avoid charismatic narcissists, with their charm and their dry hearts.

And our mother: she had had to accept that she would not have deep companionship and intimacy in her marriage. She had to accept that her children were not blessed with a loving father like hers but instead experienced daily an unempathetic parent who had no interest in them as individuals, who actually experienced them as his competitors for her attention.

Glad made do with an extremely circumscribed social life because Gil's disdain for almost everyone was a mask for his insecurity. Politically, they differed: he was a Republican, she was a Democrat. They never voted in elections because, she said, they would cancel each other out every time. Senator Joseph McCarthy was, alas, one of my father's heroes; he watched the McCarthy hearings with relish and righteousness. Mother's hero was FDR; she had listened to every fireside chat she could, and she told me she had wept when he died. Gil watched TV, Glad read books. He preferred fresh waters, she loved the ocean. In her fifties Glad developed serious heart disease. Her heavy workload, lack of exercise, her weight, and smoking were all factors. Yet the stress under our roof, year after year, also wore out her heart.

16: Latter and Last Years

Despite her health problems Gladys Ward-Dunn outlived her husband Gil by eight years. What kept her going? Her work as a physician supported her emotionally and intellectually, not just financially. She acted in the world, conducted group therapy, led teams of health workers, collaborated with colleagues on administering the large hospital. She gave talks and teaching exhibitions, served on panels.

In the course of her career she counseled and treated thousands of men, women, and children. Gil had never entered his wife's working world, never set foot in any of her offices, never drove her to a clinic, never saw her testify in court, never accompanied her to a medical conference. Over the years I have run into many people who told me how important my mother was to their relative's recovery. Fellow doctors, nurses, psychologists, and social workers who worked alongside her for years respected her and her work.

In Montreal for a medical conference, 1966. From a restaurant's souvenir matchbook cover.

On the hot June morning of my wedding day, two weeks after I graduated from college, I found my mother on her hands and knees scrubbing the worn black linoleum of our one tiny bathroom. She was in her underwear, and wiped the sweat beaded on her face as she looked up at me. What was she doing there? This was Anna's work. No, Anna was busy cooking in advance for houseguests staying after the wedding. The floor can't be that dirty, I must have said. I was very upset at seeing her labor at this menial chore in the heat on this day, she who was not in the best of health . . . *she* was important, not the floor. Seeing her looking up at me is the strongest visual memory I have of that day.

Some scenes are indelible while so much else has evaporated. My father died in April 1972, and a few weeks later Mother and I set off for London, where I was living. We had managed to expedite a passport for her, and at age sixty-four she was taking her first trip abroad. We hired a car service from Concord to Logan Airport in Boston (an extraordinary extravagance for us then). Sitting with her in the roomy backseat I read aloud Richard Brautigan's *Trout Fishing in America*. We laughed hysterically—I could hardly finish a sentence before we cracked up and couldn't stop laughing. Looking back, I think we were giving ourselves up to a strange form of grieving. We laughed until we cried.

That first night in London after our flight, Mother went to bed in my apartment on Alderney Street, SWI, and after midnight she woke me with her moaning. She could barely breathe. Soon she was in an ambulance, me too, and next I looked down a corridor and saw paddles applied to her chest and her body lift in the air. She recuperated for two weeks in Westminster Hospital, on an open ward, no private room, all expenses paid by the National Health Service. She spent a few days in the flat after her release, and my landlady (who had been personal assistant to first Nureyev, then Fonteyn) made a lovely fuss over her. I think I was able to fit in one Devon cream tea to give my mother a taste of England. Then we returned to the United States. She was deprived of the experience in England I had dreamed of for her, and I remember feeling sorry she again had been cheated of pleasure.

She healed from this heart attack, her third, and worked a few more years. Home from the office, she enjoyed preparing cocktails before dinner for the two of us when I visited. I remember her infatuation one summer with margaritas: she kept a plate with salt on the kitchen counter—for salting the rims of the stemware. Her mind had taken a very interesting turn. She had become a storyteller. Sipping her margarita, she narrated an incident, and then associated to divergent strands, one after another. Ten, twelve minutes rolled by as she wandered further afield from the original story. Then she looked at me and said with a light chuckle, "You think I don't know where I am, isn't that right?" And it's true, I was silently skeptical, and a bit worried, which she could easily read on my face. Whereupon, she deftly wove her last threads to her first, as if finishing up the most colorful knitted sock ever. It had been fifteen minutes of narrative perfection. I see now that after my father's death she relaxed in a way she never could in his presence. She could be expansive, humorous: she could be her real self.

So with my father gone and Anna living elsewhere, though still cleaning once a week, Mother invited a niece and her huge English sheepdog to live with her. She helped the young woman apply to the Katherine Gibbs School in Boston, and provided financial support. This was the continuation of her longtime educational support of her family.

When she retired from the New Hampshire State Hospital where she had worked almost twenty-five years, she announced to her colleagues that she did not want a retirement party. The younger psychiatrists who had recently joined the staff did not listen to her experiences or suggestions, and she felt demeaned, old, and shunted off. Tired, angry, and hurt, she wanted no celebration, she just wanted to go away. I was in the house the last time she walked home from Thayer Building. We were packing to move her out of the house—our house where on the doorjamb to my room Mother had penciled Mike's and my heights over all the years. I was sad for her, sad for such an end to a career where she had done so much good and had supported us so long.

I'm sitting at a little bird's-eye maple desk with curved legs and a drop-down writing leaf—which is the only piece of furniture I have from my girl-hood. All the furniture where we lived, and of course the house itself, was owned by my mother's employer, the state of New Hampshire. When she moved off the hospital grounds, she stole this desk for me. "They'll never miss it," she said. This theft was entirely out of character. I think now that she meant they wouldn't miss her.

⌀

The Kitchen Table Tells Its Tale

All senior staff shall live on the hospital grounds
in furnished housing.—NHSH Staff Manual, *1948*

A man with a half apron
fries bacon and eggs some Sundays.
He wipes me clean and enjoys his solitude.

The children are banned from the dining room.
At first they pick their pretty noses
and feed my underside. Their exile lasts for years.

A silent woman works on me.
Our day begins at 6 a.m. squeezing oranges
and ends with the last hand-dried dish, 7 p.m.

The radio murmurs in the dining room,
voices rise, a child or a crying woman leaves,
and a terrible quiet reaches me.

Saturday mornings, toast and jam for two.
The girl asks: *Why do we have to live like this.*
The mother says: *You must understand.*

The children grow up and away.
The man dies. The quiet woman leaves.
The mother decides to retire and move.

The daughter sets down the bromeliad
she's bought her mother. The plant
that can live on nothing.

No more school lunches made on me,
or cinnamon rolls, no Thanksgiving turkey,
no river bass gutted and scaled.

I have had my family life and I am done.

I will be stored in a shed, then broken up,
hauled off, burned.

Mother was going to live in a cozy apartment she had made out of an out-building attached to the somewhat rundown Victorian house my brother had bought, with her help, in the old mill town where Mike and I ran what was now our business. The last years of her life (there were six more) were dotted with dinners she and I shared an evening each week. In the first years Mike and I were business partners, I bunked in at her place, sleeping on her pull-out couch, because my apartment was seventy-five miles south in Cambridge, Massachusetts. Looking back, I realize how satisfying this time was for both of us, to be able to talk for hours on end, to enjoy each other's company.

At this time, early in her retirement, she had a recurring dream. She was amid cobwebs, empty cartons, half-filled trunks in the attic—or was it a cellar? The air was musty and dust-filled, and she was wracked with guilt: *Why hadn't she gotten out? Why did she stay? Why didn't she act?* She was revolted by her surroundings in the dream and outraged at herself for her immobility. She couldn't shake this dream; it haunted her. The derelict spaces and the immobility were emblematic of her personal life, our family life in the privacy of our home, and her regret was deep and inescapable. For all her experience as a psychiatrist, she had been powerless to deal with the gnarled and painful dynamics of our family life, she was so much a part of the drama. My father's closed-off, brittle, critical affect was virtually impossible to ameliorate.

After about four years working in what we now called "the family business," I considered changing my life. Was I meant to be working in the business in Penacook, New Hampshire? I dreamed of moving to Santa Fe, living with mountains on the horizon, the desert close by, writing, editing, making it on my own. Couldn't I still help my brother with the business long distance, with occasional trips home? I imagined telecommuting before the technology for it existed. But my mother, hearing of what was then more fantasy than plan, inveighed upon me: *Please don't leave, see me through* . . . See her through . . . her death, she meant.

In addition to heart disease Glad had diabetes and thought she was going blind. But after managing her diet and undergoing cataract surgery, she settled into enjoying Mike's children and seeing me. Two winters she flew to Florida and visited her dear friend Mary from her Philadelphia years. I wanted her

1976.

to move near me in Cambridge, but she didn't want to leave her doctors in Concord.

She started having nosebleeds and didn't tell anyone. Then on Christmas Day 1979, when she and I were having dinner together, she had another heart attack. I called the EMTs, and she started a round of hospitalizations, stabilized recovery, and further decline. "Please don't ever put me in a nursing home," she begged. But the hospital could no longer keep her and she needed round-the-clock care. It turned out she was at a nursing home only a week, but I knew I had betrayed her, though she never said that to me. Her breathing worsened and it was June when she went back to the hospital.

She was in a private room at Concord Hospital, and the nurses called her Dr. Dunn, not by her first name. She was so tired, this was the third hospitalization in two months. There was no repairing her worn heart. When I arrived one morning she sat up clear-eyed, and I knew she had been waiting for me. We chatted for a while, then from her nostrils she detached the transparent pliable tubing delivering oxygen to her system. Slowly and carefully she wound many feet of it around her lovely hand.

"I'm tired of this, it can't go on," she said to me in her clear low voice. She meant: These last six months of home, hospital, home, hospital, nursing home, hospital . . . She was putting an end to the oxygen that was keeping her alive. I knew she was competent. I was not going to argue with her: she was a doctor, it was her life, she was making a decision. She had made many decisions in her life: to go to college, to attend medical school, to work long hours treating thousands of patients, to marry, to stay in her marriage, to raise children. She did know how to make a decision.

"You're sure?"

"Oh, yes." She explained that this would take a while, and that she needed me to go off to work as if it were a normal day. Out her window, the June morning with enormous cumulus clouds and blue sky was warming. Sunlight filled the room. "I'll be fine, don't you worry." So I hugged and kissed her, told her I loved her. She lay back on the pillow and closed her eyes. I looked at her a long while from the doorway, then I left and drove to work. I could hardly believe I was in my office on such a day, in my office at my desk, talking to my brother, to others, while she lay there, doing her great work.

Now it was night, the whole hospital was quiet, and her room was dark except for a small light to the left of the bed. My brother looked in at her with her loud labor of inhaling and exhaling, and then left to hold vigil in the waiting room—hospital rooms and blood make him dizzy and faint. Listening to her deep, erratic, and ragged breathing, I stood watch with my sister-in-law, each of us holding a hand. I told my mother we were there, as if she could hear me. I knew she could not. And then, after another long while, her breathing stopped and she was gone.

Mike and his wife left. I sat in a chair in my mother's room for a time longer. I was at the elevators when the nurses who had tended her found me. They were crying too.

Last Months

For years I dreaded her flesh,
incarnation of myself in forty years,
skeins of lines, draperies,
bones showing through.
But these last months

I cannot have enough of her.
I've dreamed of lying
beside her, body
pressed to body.
My hand traces the waves
of her white hair,
my fingers stay on her arms,
I work cream into her feet.
I am glad for these hours,
for our sameness,
the line of neck,
curve of cheek,
the proud head.

Just as her flesh is failing
there is no place I will not touch,
memorizing, gathering her in.

17: Legacy from My Mother

The only hallucination I have ever had has been auditory. My mother's voice says my name. It's happened maybe five times over the last twenty years or more. It's always clear, spoken with modulation— just a naming, as if said with a smile.

If I could have ten minutes now with either of my parents, whom would I choose? If my father returned for ten minutes, personal news would be of little interest to him. He would want to know what happened to his business, and, learning what we did with it, he would not be proud of Mike and me but disgruntled that it had changed so much, that it was no longer his.

I would choose ten minutes my mother. Would I want to ask her questions? No, not anymore. As she was dying, I was alone and lost, so I would want to tell her that my life changed and turned, that I married again to a man of spiritual depth and into his wonderful family, that I bore a child, now a young man with a sunny temperament who makes music and does good work, that my brother and I made Duncraft a success, that Mike is happy each day at his desk. My fantasy is that this would delight her, even move her to conclude that all she went through was not in vain.

I could never have been who I am if not for my mother. She was the one who truly listened to me, who mirrored my true self back to me, and who was her real self with me. Just as Gladys Ward's father fostered her depth and inner resources, my mother fostered mine. She was not always present, not always attuned, but her abiding love for Mike and me, her knowing us, was crucial for developing our empathy, our range of feelings. She nurtured my independence, trusted my judgment, let me grow into myself. This is her greatest legacy.

This next legacy from my mother is subtle. As a practicing psychiatrist, of course she knew my father suffered from a severe personality disorder. However, she never discussed it with Mike or me: she let Gil Dunn stand as a strong, worthy individual with solid work. I grew up hating his behaviors but loving him; I never thought that he was sick or to be pitied, demeaned, or diminished, or that his business was "a hobby." I believe my mother knew that a strong father image was better than the image of a sick, pitiable father or the emptiness of no father in the home. And it was better for me, her daughter, to love than not love.

While my mother never had a role model of a professional woman in her youth, she provided exactly that for me. I witnessed her leave the house to perform meaningful work year in and year out. She became my template: a full-time serious career—of course I could have that. She set an example of working hard and ethically. Her example gave me a large notion of my possibilities as a woman in the world.

Lifelong interest in psychology and in dreams comes from my psychiatrist mother too. The usefulness of talking out thoughts and troubles, of exploration in therapy and in dream interpretation—these came to me naturally because of the work she did and how deeply at times we talked with each other.

It is hard for me to write about difficulties I've had because of my mother's behavior within our family circle. I so want to admire and be grateful for her. The nightmares of her last years showed me that she regretted not acting, not standing up *to* my father, not standing up *for* my brother and me. Her unconscious was hard on her: it wished, it dreamed, what was truly impossible—for her, anyway. In our day-by-day life she let Gil's roiling negativity wash around her, as if she were a rock in its stream, the rock's top surface staying dry. Sometimes she found ways to block the force of the stream from Mike and me, and sometimes she didn't. She knew she could not stop the stream, but she could prevent it from drowning us. She could manage that much, and she did. Yet my inheritance from this dynamic scenario was my own self-abnegation, patterned on hers, and depression from suppressing the anger I felt at my father's injustices and cruelties and from tamping my own responses continually. The emotional legacy from both my parents has taken years to unpack and see more clearly.

The business Mike and I took over in 1972 is as much a legacy from my mother as from my father. As a silent partner, Gladys Ward-Dunn cocreated

Duncraft; Gil's enterprise would not have lasted a year without her earnings. Her beginning salary in 1948 in New Hampshire was $5,000, and she ended her career twenty-five years later at $25,000, modest as compensation goes for medical doctors. The business, which our mother once said was my father's "hobby," grew after his death to support Mike's and my families as well as our employees, scores of individuals in the Concord area—a long-unacknowledged achievement for Gladys Ward-Dunn.

What pleasures and opportunities might she have enjoyed if her income had not flowed to the small business in Penacook? Winter trips to Florida, weekends in New York, travel in Europe, her own private practice, a house of her own on a lane in a New Hampshire village? Yet these are mostly my ideas for her. I believe she considered herself fortunate: to have become a doctor and had a medical career, to have two children and a husband, to have so much more money than in the Depression (all the clothes, shoes, and costume jewelry she could want), a live-in housekeeper, a secure job with many benefits. She drank her fill from the cup half full.

Ah, if in 1939 Gladys Ward had only discerned how thin Gil Dunn's veneer was, how impoverished his inner life, how little Gil Dunn could imagine the needs and feelings of others—she would not have made him her sweetheart, she would not have married him. She deserved love. Thirty-two, a psychiatrist, a student of the heart and mind, she never saw it coming: the freight train of flawed narcissism heading straight for her heart, straight for her remarkable life.

Pincushion

In Home Ec. class, seventh grade,
I sewed a plump pincushion
with uneven stitches, my first
creation. At twelve I was already
memorializing the past. The scrap
of fabric I had brought from home
was not ordinary. From that cloth
when I was eight my mother
sewed us matching skirts
in her precious time after work.

How proud I was: my large mother
and I, twins as we walked
downtown in woolen skirts
in maroon and green checks.
Decades later, whenever
I open the sewing box,
to sew a button, tack a hem,
the maroon and green
pincushion waits
with its little history of love.

Afterword

"Why would you want to look at your past?" a friend asked me. "Why would you want to *go* there?" he insisted.

My answer is that I wanted to stop my childhood from haunting me. I had written so many poems out of it, kept dreaming elements of it, talked about it in therapy years ago. And I still couldn't put it past me, let it rest—because I didn't understand it. How could my mid-twentieth century, middle-class childhood, with two parents, in a small city in New England "haunt" me? Our nuclear family of four looked normal, though my mother was a practicing psychiatrist, which was out of the ordinary at that time. But the walls of our home secreted a family life that was grim, contorted, and psychically painful. I felt that if I could explore this damage and understand how it came to be, how it worked, the haunting would end. The story was much larger and more complex than the fact that my father oppressed my little brother, which was the mental shorthand I had developed early on. Putting together the facts and best guesses about my parents' lives—their families, their times, and their personal struggles—I've seen what shaped them as individuals and as a couple. I understand finally why our family life was the way it was.

The father I now carry inside me has changed significantly. Once I idolized him and at times hated him. After fitting together many pieces of the puzzle of his life, I now see him as a deeply troubled and hurt soul, forever imprisoned in the many defenses constructed to protect himself from recognizing his failures, his drastic insufficiencies. His relations with each of us in the family were unique, and all served to keep his automaton "system" operating. Mother had the role of physical provider, Mike had the role of bad boy/ black sheep, and I had the role of golden good girl. I have had to face how I supplied my father with admiration and affirmation, how deeply necessary this was for him, and how in return I received dispensation from criticism and virtually nothing else. It takes my breath away in writing this to realize how the idol has crumbled.

My view of my mother has changed significantly too. Understanding how she was mothered has made me more forgiving of her shortcomings. And telling her story, I find myself deeply moved by her valor, her persistence, and her compassion. I see how much love, friendship, and society she had to forsake as she stayed in the marriage she had made.

And my brother: I see him differently too, now. Growing up, Mike never received a good word, a rough hug, a book, or an afternoon from our father. By the time he was a teen, Mike was able to see clearly, to determine, that the man we lived with was a "crazy man"—a truth I had not come to until all these years later.

One morning after finishing the two parts of this book, I dreamt a stranger came to my door with four dark dogs on four black leashes. He told me I had to take the dogs, which he had been paid to walk. I had to take responsibility for them.

I think the dogs in the dream are ghosts of four of us in my family of origin. And in this book I have been responsible for caring for and being fair to each of us. They are dark dogs, and that's why I think they are our ghosts. I take off the leashes, and before bounding off, each of the four looks back at me, and then runs free.

Sources

References, Sources

Allen, Frederick Lewis. *Only Yesterday: An Informal History of the 1920s.* New York: Harper Collins, 1964.

Bijou, Sidney W. *The Psychological Program in AAF Convalescent Hospitals.* US Army Air Force Aviation Research Reports. US Government Printing Office, 1947.

Coughlin, Robert, Jr. "Changing Roles in Modern Marriage." *Life,* December 24, 1956.

Fussell, Paul. *Wartime: Understanding and Behavior in the Second World War.* New York: Oxford University Press, 1989.

Hirshbein, Laura D. "History of Women in Psychiatry." *Academic Psychiatry* 28, no. 4 (Winter 2004): 337–43.

Huston, John, director. "Let There Be Light." US Army Pictorial Services, 1946. https://www.youtube.com/watch?v=7BZeA-tmDac.

Hymowitz, Carol, and Michaele Weissman. *The History of Women in America.* New York: Bantam, 1984.

Kelly, Orr. *Meeting the Fox: The Allied Invasion of North Africa, from Operation Torch to Kasserine Pass to Victory in Tunisia.* New York: Wiley, 2002.

Morantz-Sanchez, Regina Markell. *Sympathy and Science: Women Physicians in American Medicine.* New York: Oxford University Press, 1985.

Paine, Albert Bigelow. *Golden Cat,* with illustrations by Pelagie Doane. Philadelphia: Penn Publishing, 1934.

Reed, James E. *The Fighting 33rd Nomads During World War II: A Diary of a Fighter Pilot with Photographs and Other Stories of 33rd Fighter Group Personnel.* Vols. 1 and 2. Memphis, TN: Reed, 1988.

Ronningstam, Elsa F. *Identifying and Understanding the Narcissistic Personality.* New York: Oxford University Press, 2005.

Tuchman, Barbara. *Stilwell and the American Experience in China: 1911–1945.* New York: Macmillan, 1970.

About the Author

Sharon Dunn has published two books of poetry *Refugees in the Garden* and *My Brother and I*. For over thirty years, she with her brother in a family business in New Hampshire started by their father. She lives in Western Massachusetts and Cape Cod.

Uncollected: "Hoover Sales Office, 1939," "A Son Writes Home," "Imperatives of Body and Soul," "The Long Trip North," "In the Garden," "Pincushion"